Belli

FOR YOUR MALPRACTICE DEFENSE

FOR YOUR
MALPRACTICE
DEFENSE

Melvin M. Belli, Sr., J.D.
With John Carlova

Medical Economics Books
Oradell, New Jersey

Library of Congress Cataloging in Publication Data

Belli, Melvin M., 1907-
   Belli for your malpractice defense.

   Includes index.
   1. Physicians—Malpractice—United States. 2. Physicians—Malpractice—United States—Trial practice.
3. Trial practice—United States. I. Carlova, John.
II. Title. [DNLM: 1. Malpractice. W 44 B443b]
KF2905.3.B45   1985   346.7303'32   85-13862
ISBN 0-87489-380-1   347.306332

Art Director: Penina M. Wissner
Cover design: Fran Nimeck
Interior design: Sharyn Banks

ISBN 0-87489-380-1

Medical Economics Company Inc.
Oradell, New Jersey 07649

Printed in the United States of America

Contents

Foreword   *ix*

Publisher's Notes   *xi*

1 **How misunderstanding can generate malpractice smoke**
Even a medically competent physician can set off a legal time bomb simply by not understanding human nature.   *1*

2 **Little sparks can turn malpractice smoke into fire**
A careless remark, reluctance to listen, even a joke—any of those can compound a clinical error and make up a patient's mind to sue.   *11*

3 **Even when you win, you lose**
Losing a malpractice suit can be disastrous. Winning may not be so wonderful, either.   *19*

4 **When it's risky to refuse a patient**
Basic guidelines on free choice of patients are clear, but there are murky lanes in between that may lead you straight to court.   *23*

5 **Look out for loopholes in your malpractice policy**
Many doctors get a nasty jolt when they're sued for malpractice and find flaws in their coverage.   *27*

6 **The chilling aspects of going bare**
If you're ever tempted to practice without malpractice coverage, you'd be wise to consider the odds on taking the gamble.   *31*

7 Spotting patients likely to sue
The warning signs are there. When they start flashing,
watch out.   **35**

8 A patient's family ties can rope you into a lawsuit
In concentrating on the patient's medical needs, you just
might overlook the emotional needs of the family.   **41**

9 Is your staff leading you into legal hot water?
In the eyes of the law, the best doctor in the world is only as
good as his worst employee.   **47**

10 Guilt by association
Whether you practice alone or in a group, you can
be held liable for the acts of other doctors—in ways that
may surprise you.   **55**

11 Is your hospital a liability trap?
Many hospitals today compete rather than cooperate with
doctors. Here are the trouble areas.   **61**

12 The dangers of diagnosis
Diagnostic errors head the malpractice list. That's scary, but it
doesn't mean you should run scared.   **75**

13 The medication minefield
A drug that's wrongly prescribed can have painful side
effects for you—a session on the witness stand to explain
what went wrong.   **81**

14 Don't drop time bombs in your medical files
Good records are the keystone of a solid malpractice defense.
Bad records can blow that foundation apart.   **89**

15 How informed consent can backfire on you
A patient's consent may seem valid, but it can explode when
put to a legal test.   **95**

16 Second opinions: a growing malpractice threat
It's often helpful to obtain another doctor's opinion, but it can
be harmful if you reject it.   **103**

17 Your liability when you direct a patient to the ER
If you think you can pass along your responsibilities as well
as the patient, think again.   **107**

18 **When treating by phone calls up trouble**
The convenience of a phone can turn into a legal hazard if
you go too far. *113*

19 **The high cost of injudicious billing**
When you charge too much or press too hard for payment,
you may trigger a lawsuit. *119*

20 **When it's wise to welcome an investigation**
Many doctors instinctively resist a malpractice investigation,
but there are times when it's best to cooperate. *123*

21 **Can a private eye help you to win your case?**
Sometimes—but only if you choose the right individual; the
wrong one may make a shambles of your case. *129*

22 **Picking the right lawyer**
Whether you retain a defense attorney yourself, or your
insurance carrier assigns one, check him thoroughly.
Here's how. *135*

23 **A good way to win without going to court**
Properly handled, a deposition can work well enough to have
the case against you dropped. *139*

24 **The right way to prepare for trial**
Proper consultation with your attorney is a must, but
many other things can ease the ordeal and help your
chances of winning. *145*

25 **A good line of defense that's sometimes overlooked**
It's called contributory negligence, and it's very useful in
cases where patients themselves are at fault. *151*

26 **What you should know about expert medical witnesses**
Choosing the wrong one may do more harm than good to
your defense. *157*

27 **How to shut a "hired mouth"**
The medical expert who testifies more for pay than
principle can be a dangerous adversary—but not if you know
how to expose him. *163*

28 **Getting along with the judge**
He or she is the most powerful person in the courtroom. Forget
that, and you can forget about winning. *169*

29 **Swaying the jury to your side**
   *Individual jurors may be unpredictable, but as a group, there
   are ways you can get them to look on you with favor.*   173

30 **The importance of "show-and-tell"
   testimony**
   *The jury not only hears this evidence but sees it, which gives it
   double impact.*   179

31 **How to be a winner on the witness stand**
   *Your testimony can redeem or ruin your medical career.
   Here's expert advice on the right things to say and do.*   183

32 **What about a countersuit?**
   *This legal route is open to you under certain circumstances,
   but it's a tough road to travel.*   193

33 **The malpractice risks you'll face in
   the future**
   *Here's how to avoid future shock from medico-legal trends
   now in the formative stage.*   201

   Index   213

*F*oreword

The president of a county medical society was once asked if he'd care to meet attorney Melvin Belli.

"Why should I want to meet the devil?" the medical leader responded.

When Belli heard about this, he commented, "Well, the devil can be a very useful fellow—he can tell you how to keep out of hell. I know all about the hellfires of medical malpractice, and I understand how doctors get into them. So I can show them ways to stay out."

That, in essence, is the purpose of this book.

Belli is certainly well qualified to give advice on medicolegal matters. As a plaintiff's attorney between the 1930s and the early 1960s, he broke the medical liability field so wide open he became know as "Mr. Malpractice."

"That doesn't mean I targeted the medical profession as an enemy," Belli emphasizes. "The profession was its own worst enemy at that time. It functioned in a closely protected preserve, where incompetent doctors could literally get away with murder. Reform was badly needed, and I'd like to think I took a leading role in bringing it about."

After decades of battling doctors in court, why should Belli now want to help them?

"Well, doctors may not know it, but I come from a family line of physicians myself. If I hadn't become a lawyer, I definitely would have been a doctor. I've studied forensic medicine under some of the best specialists in the world.

"Moreover, I never enjoyed suing doctors. I like them—the good ones, at least. The fault lies with the small number of incompetents and misfits who largely cause the malpractice problem.

"Unfortunately, good doctors can fall victim to the litigious atmosphere created by bad doctors. Anyone can make a mistake, even the best of doctors. That doesn't mean it's malpractice—it just gives patients and their lawyers a peg on which to hang a malpractice suit. I've written this book to show good doctors how they can keep off that hook, or to get off it once they're on it."

Belli is practicing what he preaches. He now defends doctors in medico-legal matters, and he's a popular speaker at medical society meetings.

He also wrote a recent series of malpractice articles for Medical Economics magazine. All topped, or were close to the top of, readership surveys.

A sampling of comments from doctor-respondents: "Belli has certainly mellowed over the past 20 years"..."Excellent and instructive"..."Helps us to understand the psychology of lawyers who bring these suits"..."Although I get a knot in my stomach whenever I read an article by Belli, he is the best person to tell us how we goof."

*P*ublisher's Notes

MELVIN M. BELLI, popularly known as the "King of Torts," is a brilliant trial lawyer who has shaped and influenced the law in this country for decades. Colorful and outspoken, he has achieved fame in just about every field of legal endeavor, particularly medical malpractice.

Although much attention has been focused on Melvin Belli because of his often dramatic and innovative court presentations, he is also active in less publicized areas of the judicial scene. He is a past president of the American Trial Lawyers Association, and a founder and dean of the International Academy of Trial Lawyers.

An expert on forensic medicine, Belli is the recipient of a "Testimonial of Appreciation for Distinguished Leadership and Devotion to the Advancement of Surgical Education" from the Clinical Congress of Abdominal Surgeons. The Belli Society, an organization of 1,500 leading attorneys, sponsors seminars throughout the world on "Peace Through Law."

Belli is also a prolific author. His "Modern Trials" is a best-selling classic, and the Law Book Publishers Association has honored him "as a writer who has contributed immensely to legal literature in the 20th Century."

JOHN CARLOVA, West Coast editor of Medical Economics magazine, is the author or co-author of 14 books. His writings have appeared in The Reader's Digest, Harper's Magazine, Esquire, American Heritage, The National Geographic, and many other leading publications. He has also written for radio, television, and motion pictures.

*H*ow misunderstanding can generate malpractice smoke

Even a medically competent physician can set off a legal time bomb simply by not understanding human nature.

When doctors are sued for malpractice, they often point the finger of blame at the plaintiff's attorney. The doctor's instinctive reaction is, "That's the villain. If it weren't for him, I wouldn't be in this mess."

The malpractice problem is much more complex than that. In a 1985 report, for instance, the American Medical Association proposed that organized medicine do a better job of policing the profession to prevent incompetents from practicing. That's a fine, honest proposal, and I hope organized medicine follows through on it. Incompetent physicians, in my opinion, are the greatest cause of the malpractice problem.

What about incompetent or unscrupulous lawyers, the sort who file frivolous malpractice suits? Well, we have those, of course, and efforts are being made by responsible attorneys not only to weed them out but to block unwarranted malpractice suits before they get off the ground.

Let's start with the misapprehension that plaintiffs' lawyers file suit on behalf of anyone who comes into the office with a squawk about a doctor. That's simply not true. A good plaintiff's lawyer screens complaints very, very carefully. If a case has no merit, he's not going to win it. That means he won't get paid, and that's a terrible thing for a lawyer.

And, of course, if the lawyer doesn't adequately investigate a plaintiff's complaint, he now risks a countersuit by the doctor. So proper screening is important.

Over the years, I've encountered thousands of instances in which a patient had suffered harm—or thought he had—yet upon investigation I've had to conclude that it would be nearly impossible to win the case.

In this opening chapter, I'll explain the reasons why I sometimes drop a case before it really gets started, and what you can do to avoid similar situations.

When a patient is clearly out for revenge

This happens so often I've lost count. In most cases, it has nothing to do with medicine. A doctor can be the best clinician in the world and still set off a legal time bomb because he doesn't understand or doesn't care about human fears, lacks common courtesy, or is just plain careless. Two examples:

• The patient was a middle-aged widow, well-to-do, intelligent, but somewhat on the nervous side. For many years, she'd suffered from hypertension, which had been kept more or less under control by a succession of physicians.

The latest doctor, she complained to me, had failed to give her "proper attention." Consequently, she contended, she had suffered a minor stroke while on vacation in a distant city. She was quite angry, and she wanted to sue the doctor.

On questioning, she admitted that she had never been completely satisfied with any of her doctors, declaring, "None of them ever understood me. I was just a complaining old woman to them."

Her latest doctor, she said, was "the worst of all. He wouldn't see me himself—he'd pass me on to some nurse. He wouldn't even come to the phone when I called. Finally I told his receptionist I'd sue him unless he saw me and explained why he hadn't given me proper attention.

"He still wouldn't see me. When I told that to my family lawyer, he said, 'Well, if he won't talk to you, it might mean he knows he's done something wrong.' So I decided to get you to sue him for malpractice, Mr. Belli."

At that point, I wasn't sure whether she had a case or not. Then she made a vindictive remark that gave me pause. The doctor, she said, had made her suffer, "so now I'm going to make him suffer!"

I checked her case very carefully, and it just didn't hold up. It was true that the doctor passed her to a nurse for blood pressure tests, but that's routine in many medical offices. His care of her, in all clinical respects, was up to standard, and there certainly was no negligence—at least not medically.

The doctor *was* negligent, though, in failing to heed the red flags flying all over this lady. She was demanding; she was a doctor-shopper and a chronic complainer; she had emotional needs that went far beyond her clinical problem; and she was litigious.

Most of this must have been obvious to the doctor. He had a choice: He could have given the patient more attention, or if he hadn't the time and inclination to do that, he could have gracefully persuaded her to try another doctor. Instead, he turned away. That's when she set out for revenge. Although no suit was ever filed, the doctor could have saved himself a very unsettling experience if he had just used a little common sense.

● An architect was hospitalized for a colostomy. He had

been assured by one of the four doctors involved in his case that he'd be out of the hospital in a couple of weeks. Instead, because of intestinal blockage and other complications, his stay lasted six weeks.

He eventually came to me with a complaint against all four doctors. They were incompetent and negligent, he declared, and he wanted to sue them "for every penny they've got." Later, he bitterly added, "Doctors are money-grabbers. They've got dollar signs where their brains should be. So the only way we can get back at them is to hit them right in their pocketbooks."

There were two reasons for the patient's decision to sue, I learned upon investigation. (1) He felt he had been "promised" that he'd be out of the hospital much sooner than the six weeks he had to stay. (2) While he was still in the hospital, he received a dunning letter from one of his doctors, demanding payment of a $525 bill.

As far as medical care was concerned, however, my investigation showed that the doctors had done their job. The complications that arose weren't their fault.

The doctor who had assured the patient he'd be in the hospital only a few weeks had done so, he told me, "because the patient was worried and depressed, and I was just trying to cheer him up." That's kind, but it's unwise to guarantee or warrant anything relating to a cure.

The doctor who'd sent the patient the dunning letter claimed that "one of my assistants just got too zealous. I didn't know what was going on."

Well, he should have known, because a doctor bears responsibility for what his employees do. Many malpractice suits have been set in motion by discourteous receptionists, unfeeling nurses, or even sloppy answering services.

When the patient goes against medical advice
Malpractice plaintiffs are quick to claim incompetence in doctors, but somewhat slower to admit failings of their own.

Therefore, when such failings come to the attention of a doctor during treatment, he'd be wise to put them on record.

One patient, for instance, was a heavy drinker. His family physician repeatedly warned him to cut down on the booze, but to no avail. Eventually the patient had to undergo emergency surgery. He died on the operating table.

Later the family came to me, all set to sue the surgeon and the primary physician. They made no mention of the patient's heavy drinking. I learned about that from the primary physician, but he had no documentation, just his word that he had warned the patient of the ills of overindulging. When it later came out that the patient had openly bragged to friends about ignoring the doctor's warnings, the case was dropped.

On another occasion, I was asked to sue the doctor of a man who'd died of a coronary. The doctor, however, had records of the numerous times he'd advised the patient to go on a low-sodium diet, lose some of his excess weight, and eliminate the martinis from his daily routine. He'd even sent a letter of warning to the patient, whose only response was to tell the doctor, "To hell with it—I feel fine."

I turned that one down in a hurry.

When the doctor can't control the result

A few years ago, I was retained to represent a family in a wrongful death suit against a GP. The patient was a 37-year-old woman who had died while under treatment for an inflamed appendix.

I was still investigating the case when I received a phone call from the GP. In a determined voice, he said he wanted to come over and explain to me exactly what had happened.

Now, that's unusual. Defense lawyers generally warn their clients to stay as far away as they can from the plaintiff's attorney. Puzzled but interested, I put the doctor on hold, called his lawyer, and asked what was going on. He told me the GP felt so strongly that he'd done nothing wrong that he insisted on seeing me.

So I got back to the GP and told him, sure, come on over. He turned out to be a down-to-earth fellow who believed in tackling his problems head-on. I listened, and was impressed.

He started at the beginning and went over the entire course of the patient's treatment. As far as I could tell, the doctor had taken care to do all the right things. He explained that the patient had fallen victim to a blood impurity that had caused a toxic reaction—something beyond a doctor's control.

The doctor's records were impeccable, and I had no doubt he could get plenty of expert witnesses to back him up. I had to tell the family they had no case.

That isn't always easy. Too many people have the impression that they can win a malpractice case simply on the basis of injury or death. That isn't enough, of course, as I explained in this instance. Unless negligence can be proved, there's no cause for action.

When a complaint is based on a misunderstanding

If the doctor is busy and the patient is confused or frightened, a breakdown of communication can occur. That can lead to litigation.

I recall one case in which a young woman was brought to a hospital to deliver her first baby. The delivery presented no problems, but the woman and her husband left the hospital angry.

They later came to me and wanted to sue the doctor for what they called his callous behavior, incompetence, and total indifference. The way they told it, the doctor hadn't come to the woman until shortly before the birth, and he never contacted the husband in the waiting room afterward.

This, they said, had caused them both physical and emotional distress. They'd been told by many people, they went on, that the doctor who delivers the baby is supposed to be on the spot well in advance to attend to the mother and communicate with the father.

That isn't always so, of course, but I checked their story. As it turned out, the attending physician—a highly qualified man—had been called in an emergency to assist in another, complicated birth. However, he had delegated two trained OB nurses to look after the young woman, and her care was far better than standard. There was no way the doctor could have successfully been sued.

The point here is that the doctor could have averted even the threat of a suit by communicating to the fearful young woman what had happened, then passed similar word to the anxious father in the waiting room.

When a decision is made under extraordinary circumstances

Just about all courts make allowances for such circumstances. Therefore, a prudent plaintiff's attorney will closely scrutinize cases with extraordinary situations before moving into the legal system with them.

I remember an old rancher who came to me, complaining about a doctor who'd treated him for snakebite. The treatment, he claimed, had been worse than the bite, and the physician hadn't warned him of the extreme side effects that came with the treatment.

Well, I pulled out a law book and read to the rancher an appellate court ruling that stated it was not necessary for a physician to discuss possible consequences and methods of treatment with a snakebite victim "while the venom is being pumped through the patient's body."

The rancher pondered that a while, then he nodded, stood up, and summarized the situation: "I guess you have to pay some price for having your life saved, eh, Mel?"

"Yeah," I said, "especially if it's in an emergency."

"Just the same," the rancher went on, "that doctor should have told me about those goddam side effects."

I had to agree with that, and the rancher nodded again and left. I heard no more about a lawsuit.

When one doctor bad-mouths another

This used to be a common problem, and it still happens. A typical example: A woman had minor surgery done by a GP. It left a scar. Later, on the advice of a friend, she went to a board-certified surgeon, who asked her, "Who did this?" When she told him, he shook his head and muttered, "I know that guy—still practicing Stone Age medicine."

The woman then came to me, inquiring about the possibility of suing the GP. Before committing myself, I called the surgeon, explained the situation, and asked if he'd back up his remark about the GP in court.

"Absolutely not!" he immediately responded. "First of all, I don't recall making such a remark. Second, any discussion I had with the patient was private and confidential. Forget it!"

And that's what usually happens in these cases. For whatever reason, a doctor will question the skill or knowledge of another, then refuse to testify in court. Unless outside expert medical testimony can be obtained, there's just no case.

I must say, though, that doctors today are much more willing to testify as expert witnesses against other doctors than they were in the bad old days of the conspiracy of silence. When I started in practice, the only expert medical witness I could get was "Sew-em-up" Smith, a worn-out little old GP who could, and frequently did, disprove the notion that a quart will not go into a pint container.

Well, the defense lawyer would get up and say something like, "Imagine an old reprobate like Smith testifying against my good and glorious Dr. So-and-so! It's a shame!"

And I'd get up and say to the jury, "Yes, it is a shame. In fact, it's downright shocking, because I can't get any other doctor to testify against the good and glorious Dr. So-and-so." And, gradually, juries began to agree with me that it was indeed shocking.

It wasn't much later that the conspiracy of silence we attorneys had long complained about began to break down. With that, medicine ceased to function as a mystical, indisputable force and moved closer to the heart of society. I think both medicine and society have been the better for that.

When a patient hits back at an "insensitive" doctor

These cases are rare, but several have come to my attention, and you should know about them. They're based not on medical negligence but thoughtless behavior by the doctor. The legal theory is that the doctor's insensitivity to the patient's feelings exacerbated the illness and hindered recovery.

No court has yet ruled on this sort of case, but the warning is clear: In addition to providing good clinical care, doctors may be held to higher standards of dealing personally with patients. A couple of examples as reported by Jack E. Horsley, a leading malpractice defense attorney based in Illinois:

• A middle-aged man was hospitalized for repeated anginal episodes. Several doctors were involved in his care, and they managed to control the angina.

On the eve of the patient's discharge, one of the doctors came in to check him out. The doctor was in a bad mood, and he finally got fed up with the patient's griping about restrictions on his activities and diet.

"Your heart is telling you something!" the doctor shouted. "Are you too stupid to hear it?"

Shocked speechless, the patient just stared at the doctor. Later that night, though, he suffered a major heart attack that forced him to remain in the hospital another two weeks.

Subsequently, the patient filed a suit seeking compensation from the doctor and the hospital for the extra expense of hospitalization, plus pain, emotional distress, and punitive damages. The case was settled in favor of the patient for an undisclosed sum.

• This patient was a 60-year-old woman who had been hospitalized for cirrhosis of the liver. It was known to the two doctors in the case that she had long been a secret, heavy drinker.

One evening, the two doctors were at the bedside of the patient, along with her husband, a railroad executive. One doctor, in the course of conversation, remarked, "I can't understand how she managed to get all that booze without someone getting wise to her."

This caused the husband to blow up, and soon he and the offending doctor were yelling at each other. The violent quarrel upset the woman so much that she had to undergo psychiatric treatment and stay longer in the hospital than expected.

Afterward, she and her husband filed suit against the two treating physicians. The suit was later abandoned by the husband when the woman died of causes other than cirrhosis of the liver.

In the old days, a doctor could lose his temper and berate the hell out of a patient, and the patient would meekly take it. He or she wouldn't dream of standing up to such an authority figure. Now patients are not only standing up, they're talking of suing.

If a case of this sort should be won in trial and upheld on appeal, new law would be established, opening up a floodgate of new legal problems for "insensitive" doctors.

However, that's in the future. Right now, in the next chapter, let's look at what happens when a doctor makes a clinical mistake and compounds it with another sort of blunder.

2

*L*ittle sparks can turn malpractice smoke into fire

A careless remark, reluctance to listen, even a joke—any of those can compound a clinical error and make up a patient's mind to sue.

It started as a routine procedure. The patient, a middle-aged woman, had awakened in the night with vertigo, which frightened her. She was still obviously worried as she described her symptoms to a young family physician.

"What bothers me the most," she complained, "is this terrible dizziness."

"Well, don't worry," the doctor told her. "We get a lot of dizzy dames around here."

The woman was not amused. "I don't think that's funny!" she retorted. "This is a serious problem. I've been thinking all sorts of things, even that I might have a brain tumor."

"Oh, nonsense," said the doctor. "Actually, it's probably only wax impacted in your ears."

He was right. In removing the wax, though, the doctor scraped an ear canal, which subsequently caused the woman some pain.

Ordinarily, that would hardly have been grounds for a malpractice suit. The woman, however, was still smarting from the "dizzy dame" remark, and she filed suit. Ultimately, it was settled out of court for a small sum.

The point here is that the doctor probably could have avoided all the anxiety and hassle of litigation if he had used discretion in handling the patient. Humor is sometimes useful in putting a patient at ease, but if it's heavy-handed or ill-timed, the bitter joke may well be on the doctor.

The fact is that most malpractice cases are won by defendant doctors. That's because negligence must be proved, which isn't easy in most instances. Sometimes, though, an emotional element will be introduced that can make a simple clinical mistake *seem* like negligence—at least, to a judge, a jury, or a malpractice insurance carrier.

Poking fun at a patient is one way of creating that unfavorable impression. Here are others.

Ignoring the patient

She was a difficult patient, and she complained repeatedly to her doctor about painful side effects from various medications he prescribed to bring down her high blood pressure. Finally she wrote a letter to the doctor, accusing him of incompetence and threatening to find another physician. He filed it without answering, figuring it was just another crank letter.

About a month later, the woman died of a massive stroke, and her family sued the doctor for malpractice. The doctor's "indifference," they claimed, had directly led to the woman's death.

Her letter to the doctor was introduced as an indication of the stress she was under. Also, the doctor admitted in a deposition that he had not answered the woman, and in fact was "glad to get rid of her."

The impact of all this on a jury was anticipated by the doctor's malpractice carrier, which settled the case.

Even if patients are not hostile, it's risky to ignore them. Examples:

• The doctor in this case was the strong silent type. He preferred to keep conversation with patients to a minimum. That's fine if the doctor feels it assists his concentration and saves time. If it worries the patient, though, look out for trouble.

In this instance, the patient was a stockbroker who suspected he had heart disease. During the examination, he asked a number of questions. The doctor responded only with a grunt.

Finally the patient inquired, "How's it going, Doctor? Is everything all right?"

In exasperation, the doctor halted the examination and bluntly told the patient, "I can't do my job if you keep gabbing away. Now keep quiet or find a doctor who'd rather talk than properly examine you."

The patient shut up, but several weeks later he suffered a heart attack. In a subsequent malpractice suit, he accused the doctor of failing to diagnose his condition and "aggravating that condition by abusive language."

In deposition, several patients who were in the waiting room told of overhearing the doctor's outburst. Realizing the effect this would have on a jury, the doctor's malpractice insurance carrier induced him to settle out of court.

Moral: When an anxious patient asks questions, the wise doctor will realize the need for communication and respond accordingly.

• Alfred Julian, a capable New York plaintiff's attorney, recalls a medical malpractice complaint that was brought to him by a woman who'd undergone a dermabrasion by a doctor's office nurse. The result was unsatisfactory, and the patient was unable to contact the doctor. He wouldn't see her, and he refused calls from her.

"I didn't think it was a problem that required court action," comments Julian. "So I wrote the doctor a letter, saying I'd been offered this case and was considering it, but that I also thought a face-to-face meeting might clear the air. He saw her—and promised to redo the work himself. That was the last I heard of the case, except for a thank you letter from the relieved doctor to me."

Julian sums up: "I've seen a lot of malpractice cases generated because of the patient's inability to reach the doctor when something goes wrong. A doctor shouldn't hide behind receptionists or refuse phone calls. A good face-to-face talk can often head off a nasty complaint."

I couldn't agree more.

Talking tough

I'm well aware of the need for doctors to develop a protective shield—otherwise they might crack up under the physical and emotional rigors of practicing medicine. I'm amazed at times, however, by the sheer heartlessness, or thoughtlessness, of some doctors' comments to patients.

In one case, the woman patient feared injections.

"Don't be such a baby!" the doctor scolded her. "Hold still and let's get on with it. I've never bungled an injection yet."

This time he did. The injection site became infected, and injury ensued from sloughing of the tissue.

The damage wasn't great, but the woman filed a malpractice suit—largely, she later disclosed, because of the doctor's "tough-guy" talk. The case was settled for $28,500.

In another case, the plaintiff was represented by Bruce Walkup, a San Francisco plaintiff's attorney. The suit stemmed from the medical treatment of a mother of six children. It started one evening when she experienced abdominal cramps and syncope.

Her husband phoned a local doctor and asked him to come over.

"Can you afford to pay for a house call?" the doctor asked.

"Of course—just get over here."

After briefly examining the woman, the doctor gave her shots of penicillin and Demerol.

Later, the woman's cramps increased. Unable to reach the local doctor, the husband tried to get his wife admitted to a nearby hospital but was told he had to obtain a physician's approval.

The doctor finally phoned the next day and instructed the husband to pick up some Empirin with Codeine tablets at the hospital. The woman vomited after taking the tablets, and the husband took her to the ER. She died there from a ruptured tubal pregnancy.

During the trial for wrongful death, Walkup put the father of the deceased woman on the stand and asked him to describe what happened when the doctor arrived at the hospital after the death of the patient.

"He lifted the sheet off my daughter."

"Did he make any comment?"

"Well, sir," replied the father, "he said, 'Here today, gone tomorrow. We've all got to go sometime.'"

That remark was the clincher. The jury voted against the doctor.

The moral is extremely clear: Tough talk can have tough consequences.

Giving way to pressure

Many dedicated doctors have a common failing—they take on more work than they can properly handle. Another type of doctor goes beyond his skills in treating patients, thus putting additional strains on himself. In either case, the pressure can result in a blowout. A typical example:

An overworked FP cut down on the amount of time he spent with each patient, and gave short shrift to those he thought were hypochondriacs.

On one occasion, after examining a woman who complained of persistent headaches, he snapped at her, "You're imagining a lot of stuff. Take some aspirin. If that doesn't work, check back with me. Right now I have a lot of really sick people waiting to see me."

Two nights later, the woman awoke with a particularly painful headache. At a hospital ER, she was referred to a neurologist, who found the woman had a cerebral tumor. Surgery was performed, but it was too late. She died.

When the husband filed a malpractice suit, the FP's insurance carrier didn't even consider going to court. "The emotional factors involved were just too great, especially the doctor's unfeeling remark to the patient," says an attorney with close knowledge of the suit. "The case was settled for an amount well into six figures."

And it all might have been avoided if the FP had recognized his limitations in time and expertise.

Carelessness in reporting tests

When a patient comes to a doctor with a suspected disease—especially a dread disease—the anxiety level is high. Unfortunately, some doctors break bad news the wrong way.

In reporting a lab test, for example, an internist bluntly told a woman patient, "Well, the worst has happened—you have cancer of the breast. You waited too long for this test."

The woman fainted. Revived, she kept screaming, "I'm going to die! I'm going to die!"

She didn't die, but an operation on her breast had painful aftereffects. The internist was included in a subsequent malpractice suit because, the patient claimed, he had caused her "great and unnecessary mental anguish."

That particular claim might or might not have stood up in court, but the internist's carrier figured it would be less costly to settle for a few thousand dollars.

The internist's malpractice premium was then doubled, showing how an indiscreet choice of words can be costly.

In a similar case, another woman went to a doctor with suspected breast cancer. The mammogram appeared to be nega-

tive, so the doctor told the patient, "Forget about breast cancer. You don't have it."

This relieved the woman's anxiety, but her husband wasn't
satisfied. He took her to another doctor, who did find breast
cancer. Later, the woman sued the first doctor for failing to
diagnose the malignancy.

The original mammogram, it turned out, had been equivo-
cal. In interpreting it, the doctor had erred in trying to ease
the patient's anxiety with a good report. He should, of course,
have tested further. Tests are generally accurate diagnostic
tools, but they're not infallible.

An over-optimistic report on tests, in fact, can sometimes
lead to complications of another sort. For example, when a
patient was told he had lung cancer, he asked the doctor, "Are
you sure?"

"Well, that's what the tests show. Anyway, don't worry
about it—we detected it early."

"Does that mean you can get it all out?"

"Possibly. Relax—take it easy."

As it turned out, surgery failed to remove all of the cancer.
The malignancy spread, the patient died, and the family sued
the doctor. Part of the complaint read, "The doctor guaranteed a cure."

Actually, the doctor hadn't guaranteed a cure, yet by feed-
ing the patient's great expectations, he inadvertently *implied* a
guarantee. The case was finally dismissed, but only after several years of litigation.

Even when a physician wins a suit of this sort, it's a hollow
victory. I'll explain why in the next chapter.

*E*ven when you win, you lose

3

Losing a malpractice suit can be disastrous. Winning may not be so wonderful, either.

Don't think the only cost of a malpractice suit is in money.

In a recent study of 154 physicians who had been defendants, a majority suffered from depression or other psychosomatic illnesses, and 8 percent actually came down with physical ailments.

Nearly 20 percent reported a "loss of nerve" in some clinical situations after the suit had been resolved. Fifteen percent said they'd lost confidence in themselves as physicians.

These are pretty scary figures, yet many doctors don't fully realize what the impact of a malpractice suit can be. That's why I've particularly designed this book to help doctors to avoid even the *appearance* of negligence. I've laid down guidelines that, if followed, will help physicians stay out of malpractice situations, even winnable ones—for "winnable" is an ironic term in this context. For example:

A doctor friend of mine, a leading specialist in his field, once remarked to me, "I practice good medicine and I keep

19

meticulous records, so the odds are in my favor if I'm ever sued for malpractice. I'll win."

He was right. He was sued and he won, but he came out of the experience a very bitter man. The very fact that he'd been dragged through well-publicized hearings prior to his day in court cast a shadow on his reputation; he had to pay out thousands of dollars of his own money to supplement his insurance coverage; his professional and private lives were disrupted; and he came out of it all with a deep distrust of patients, warily viewing them as prospective plaintiffs.

Too many doctors have the overly optimistic attitude that my friend used to have. They're misled by figures showing that physicians win the majority of malpractice suits brought against them. They're confident they practice good medicine and feel it would be difficult for a plaintiff to prove negligence, proximate cause, and measurable injury—three elements needed to successfully support a complaint.

What they may not realize is the destruction that even an unwarranted suit can inflict on a doctor. Even a "victory" takes a high toll in time and energy.

In New Jersey, for instance, a cardiologist was sued for $4 million by a patient he'd never seen or treated. The case was ultimately dismissed, but it took the cardiologist two long and anxious years to get the mess cleared up.

Trial dates were set and postponed; sleepless nights became the norm for the doctor; his days were disrupted by interrogatories, hearings, depositions, and telephone calls relative to the suit; and he had to work long and hard on a defense that amounted to "a semester's worth of teaching cardiology" before the plaintiff grudgingly admitted he'd been mistaken and agreed to a dismissal.

In a similar instance, a family physician was baffled by a suit charging him with malpractice in a hospital emergency room where he'd never practiced. The complaint was bizarre. It contained 41 defendants, all identified as Doe except the FP, who couldn't even figure out what he was accused of. He finally found that he was supposed to have botched a procedure that he'd never performed in his whole career.

To make matters worse, the FP was covered by two malpractice insurers. There was a prolonged dispute over which policy applied in this case and which company would defend the doctor—or, more worrisome, not defend him.

When that was straightened out, the doctor had to travel 150 miles to attend a deposition arranged by the plaintiff's lawyer. After two hours of questioning, the doctor was allowed to introduce records and evidence, including an old calendar, that proved he'd been camping with friends when the alleged malpractice occurred.

"Well, Doctor," the lawyer conceded, "I can see you're an honest man."

The same could hardly be said for the lawyer. Apparently he hadn't been sure about who to name in the complaint. He only knew the last name of the doctor who was supposed to have performed the botched procedure. So the lawyer went through the county medical society directory and found five doctors with the same last name. He then picked the one at the top of the list—which happened to be the FP—added 40 John Does for good measure, and fired off his shotgun case.

The lawyer's behavior, of course, was outrageous, and the FP has quite rightly countersued him.

Even a countersuit, though, cannot always correct matters. In California, a woman doctor was driven out of a thriving practice by slanderous remarks made about her by a patient who had sued for malpractice. The malpractice action was eventually dropped, and the doctor won a $100,000 countersuit for malicious prosecution. By then, however, a decade had passed since the malpractice suit was filed, and the doctor was working in a salaried state job with no hope of getting back into private practice.

What can doctors do to avoid, or alleviate, such disasters? The main safeguard is to be aware of how your daily contacts with patients, patients' families, your office assistants, your

medical associates, and the hospitals you practice in can land
you in legal trouble, even when you've done no wrong yourself. With this awareness, you can be prepared to stay out of
trouble, or deal effectively with it if it happens. We'll go into
all of that in chapters to come.

Let's deal first, however, with the notion that you can pick
and choose your patients as you please.

4

When it's risky to refuse a patient

Basic guidelines on free choice of patients are clear, but there are murky lanes in between that may lead straight to court.

One reason I like doctors is that they're individualistic. They think for themselves, and they take pride in their independence. That's fine, except that sometimes they believe they have more professional freedom than they actually possess.

Consider the dictum from the AMA Principles of Medical Ethics that states, "Physicians are free to choose whom they will serve." Some doctors take that too literally, not knowing that certain qualifiers open up the possibility of a lawsuit.

Qualifier number one is: "The physician should, however, respond to the best of his ability in cases of emergency where first-aid treatment is essential."

Number two: "Once having undertaken a case, the physician should not neglect the patient, nor withdraw from the case without giving notice to the patient, the relatives, or responsible friends sufficiently long in advance of withdrawal to permit another medical attendant to be secured."

We're not talking here about Good Samaritan emergency situations that occur away from medical offices and hospitals. Doctors are pretty well covered by law when they go to the aid of someone in those cases.

However, if a stranger stumbles into your office, says he's ill, and asks for medical help, another situation arises. He's not a patient, he appears drunk, you're busy and don't want to be bothered. You tell your receptionist to get rid of the guy, who drops dead of a heart attack outside your office.

Can you be held liable? Probably. Can you base a successful defense on the fact that you're "free to choose" whom you will serve? Probably not.

Basically, a doctor has a duty to give immediate first-aid treatment in an emergency of this sort. Afterward, if the doctor feels he can do no more, he should have the patient transferred as soon as possible to the nearest ER or other medical facility. Any doctor who does less will almost surely be looked upon unkindly by a jury.

Does the provision of first-aid treatment commit the physician to an ongoing patient-doctor relationship? No, although some physicians shy away from treating an emergency patient for that reason.

Do you have the right to refuse patients who are on welfare or are uninsured? Yes, but make sure you inform your staff that a medical emergency is an exception to this rule. If one of your staff turns away someone in medical need just because he can't pay, a courtroom will be a very unfriendly place for you.

Let's turn now to the related issue of abandonment. One court defines it as "a failure by the physician to continue to provide service to the patient when it is still needed in a case for which the physician has assumed responsibility and from which he has not been relieved."

In an emergency situation such as we've been describing, such relief would usually come when the doctor has discharged his duty to provide first-aid treatment and anything else that's immediately necessary.

In other cases, the physician's responsibility begins when the doctor-patient relationship is established and it ends when care is no longer needed. This raises the question: When can you safely assume that care is no longer needed?

Well, let's say a patient comes to you with a complaint about a sore throat. Then it develops that he has more than one complaint—he gripes about everything, including your methods of treatment, and you get fed up with him. If you dismiss him before that sore throat is cured, he can accuse you of abandonment. But if you wait until the problem is cleared up, you can safely tell the patient to clear out.

Do it diplomatically, of course. Suggest he'd probably be more compatible with another doctor, and direct him to your local medical society for a list of physicians qualified to meet his medical needs. To safeguard yourself, make a note of the discharge in the patient's medical record, and send him a letter of confirmation.

What if the patient discharges *you?* That ends the doctor-patient relationship, but again, safeguard yourself by sending the patient a letter confirming the break, and by keeping a copy on file.

There are other circumstances in which you can safely assume you've been discharged. If the patient ignores your advice, doesn't keep appointments for treatment, or leaves a hospital against your advice, he loses his right to continuous care from you.

In any event, *before* you get into a malpractice situation, you'd be wise to check your malpractice policy for such tricky legalese as "duty to cooperate," "ultimate net loss," and "pure loss coverage." These terms may not mean what you think, as you'll discover in the next chapter.

5

*L*ook out for loopholes in your malpractice policy

Many doctors get a nasty jolt when they're sued for malpractice and find flaws in their coverage.

A lot of people come into my office with legal problems, and the first thing they say is, "I didn't read the contract," or, "I read it but I didn't understand it."

Well, a malpractice insurance policy is a contract, and a doctor should be absolutely sure he understands it *before* trouble strikes. Otherwise, the insurance carrier can say, "Well, you didn't abide by the terms of our agreement, so we're not going to pay off."

That could spell financial disaster for the doctor. Even if he won the case, he'd have to shell out the defense costs, which could run up to $50,000 or more.

To avoid that sort of disaster, here's what you should do:

• Go over the policy carefully, item by item. If you don't understand the fine print, call in someone who does—either a contract lawyer, or an insurance broker who has a solid background in analyzing insurance policies.

• Whether you check the policy yourself or someone else does it for you, find out if you're covered for all claims arising during the policy term.

"Claims made" insurance, for example, covers only claims, or notices of possible claims, that are *reported* during the policy period. "Occurrence" coverage, on the other hand, insures all claims arising from the time the policy was in force, no matter when those claims are filed, and that might be years after the policy expires.

"Claims made" insurance is cheaper, but "occurrence" is a better deal, if you can get it. If you can't, buy separate "tail" coverage when the claims made policy ends. This will protect you against future claims stemming from that period.

• If you're in group practice, be certain you're clear about the coverage for each member and the group as a whole.

A four-member group, for example, figured that because they had $2 million coverage for each member, the overall amount would be $8 million. Therefore, when they were recently hit as a group by a malpractice case, they were shocked to learn from the carrier that the overall coverage was only $2 million. The loophole was in fine print that said if the group was named in a malpractice suit, and if all members were served with complaints, only one limit would apply.

That clause is questionable, of course, but the doctors may have waited too long to question it.

• Don't be confused by "pure loss" and "ultimate net loss." If you get the wrong one in your policy, you could wind up thousands of dollars out of pocket.

That happened to a partnership of two oncologists sued by a woman they'd treated for stage IV cervical cancer. They saved the patient's life, but she complained that radiation damaged her ureter and rectum.

The verdict in the case was in favor of the oncologists. Yet because their policy was written for pure loss coverage, they had to fork over $5,000 of the defense lawyer's fee. If the policy had specified ultimate net loss, the carrier would have paid all legal costs.

• Be aware of your "duty to cooperate." When you see that in your policy, it means you're expected to help the insurer to handle a claim. That may seem reasonable enough, but it's not always so. Consider the following case:

When a surgeon was sued for malpractice, the carrier assigned to the case an attorney who was unsure about how to deal with the problems involved. As a result, he called on the surgeon repeatedly for conferences, depositions, and hearings. The surgeon finally complained that his practice and private life were suffering.

The attorney responded by threatening to have the surgeon's coverage cancelled.

"On what grounds?" the doctor demanded.

"On the grounds that you aren't fulfilling your duty to cooperate," the attorney replied.

The surgeon then retained a lawyer and put the matter to a legal test. The main contention made by the lawyer, who specialized in medico-legal matters: The insurance company attorney was asking for too much cooperation. Ultimately, the carrier agreed, and a more knowledgeable attorney was assigned to the case.

In sum, "duty to cooperate" is so broad a term that it can occasionally be applied in a questionable way. Generally, though, it's in a doctor's best interest to comply with reasonable requests by the carrier to cooperate.

• Don't miss a time limit on reporting a claim.

This is a failing of quite a few doctors who get into difficulties with insurance carriers. For whatever reason, the doctor just shoves the malpractice claim out of sight.

"I was busy," is one common explanation, or, "It got lost in some other papers," or, "I wanted to think about it."

Well, it's the job of insurance experts to "think about" claims, and the sooner the better.

Some policies set a specific time limit on claims, others simply say "promptly." Play it safe: Report a claim as soon as you receive it. Otherwise, you may get a shock when the insurance company says, "You didn't report it on time, so we're entitled to cancel coverage."

- Don't try to cut corners on "full disclosure."

In a recent case, a physician was accused of malpractice because he'd neglected a hospitalized patient. Among the questions put to him by his carrier-assigned attorney was, "Have you ever been denied hospital privileges anywhere, or have you ever lost such privileges?"

The doctor's answer: "Never."

On trial, however, the doctor was forced by the plaintiff's lawyer to admit that he had in fact been denied privileges at an out-of-state hospital. He lost the case, and the carrier is now disputing payment of the award because the physician failed to make full disclosure.

The term itself, I know, is somewhat ambiguous, but you can generally safeguard yourself by telling the truth, the whole truth, and nothing but the truth. Don't think that this sort of truth is reserved for the courtroom—your malpractice insurance carrier is entitled to it, too.

But what if you don't have a malpractice insurance carrier? We'll tackle that question in the next chapter.

6

The chilling aspects of going bare

If you're ever tempted to practice without malpractice insurance, you'd be wise to consider the odds on taking the gamble.

A few years ago, I was involved in a medical malpractice trial that resulted in a $1.5 million verdict against a doctor. He had no insurance coverage, so he just disappeared. Later we learned he'd vanished into the jungles of lower Mexico, which may be an interesting place to visit but is hardly the ideal spot to spend the rest of one's life.

That's just one example of how doctors can lose heavily when they go bare, which in my opinion is like playing Russian roulette with your career.

I have professional liability coverage myself, and I'm damn glad I do. Not too long ago, I was hit with a $46 million suit for legal malpractice. The jury returned a verdict in my favor, but it was a long and emotionally arduous ordeal. I hate to think what might have happened if I lost and *didn't* have professional liability insurance.

It's understandable, though, how some doctors fall into this trap. I know of a family physician who dropped his coverage because he'd never been sued and felt his premiums had soared too high. A few years later, one of his patients, a show business celebrity, died under mysterious circumstances, and the FP was sued by the family for wrongful death.

For three years, he suffered sleepless nights and anxious days. He feared not only that he'd be walloped with a hefty malpractice award—which would have wiped him out financially—but that the publicity of a trial of this sort would mark him forever.

When the case finally came to trial, however, the media missed it because the celebrity was identified under her real name rather than her theatrical name. Moreover, the jury returned a verdict in favor of the doctor.

But was he really a winner? Hardly. His lawyer's fees were $20,000, and he dropped thousands more in time lost from his practice.

Incidentally, he now has malpractice coverage.

Another uninsured doctor was a bigger loser. He also had never been a victim of a malpractice complaint. Then lightning struck three times in a row. The doctor won all of the suits, but lost $100,000 because of triple court costs.

Let's look at another side of the going-bare picture. Isn't it possible that an uninsured doctor could lose a malpractice case and still turn out to be a winner financially because of savings over the years in not paying high premiums? Sure, but there are drawbacks to that, too.

Take a group of specialists who decided during the malpractice insurance crisis of the mid-1970s to dispense with their big-bucks coverage. Six years later, in a one-in-a-million mishap, they landed in a real malpractice mess. A woman who had come to the group for treatment to facilitate birth was mistaken for another patient who was due for an abortion. Result: The woman who fervently wanted a baby was presented with a dead fetus.

The patient and her husband sued the group for $1 million. A jury awarded the couple $200,000, which looked like a good deal for the group—it was less than they would have paid over the years in insurance premiums. The $200,000, however, came out of a reserve fund set up to expand the group's facilities. That had to be put off.

Furthermore, group morale dropped. The doctor who had aborted the wrong patient admitted after the trial that he had suffered near disabling insecurity during the long and painful ordeal.

"For the first time in my career," he said, "the practice of medicine became a burden. Since every decision had to be infallible, I found myself double-checking on assistants and colleagues whose work I'd trusted for years. The tension was nearly unbearable."

The head of the group added: "We practiced good medicine before the incident, but we may have become overconfident. Now we're shaken. We've seen how easy it is to slip up. We wouldn't think of continuing in practice without malpractice coverage."

Three other things to keep in mind:

1. **The unappealing aspects of an appeal.** Say you win a case, but the plaintiff takes it to a higher court. That means further financial outlay in lawyers' fees and court costs—often as much as the $25,000 to $30,000 outlay for the original trial. And, of course, if the plaintiff wins the appeal, you're right back where you started—only a lot poorer.

2. **The unsettling part of a settlement.** When a malpractice insurance company spots a difficult case to defend, a settlement is quickly sought and reached. It's usually the less expensive way to go.

An uninsured doctor, however, no matter how affluent he may be, can be financially jarred by a settlement that ranges up to six or more figures.

3. **How going bare can turn away patients and alienate your colleagues.** Once word gets around that a doctor is unin-

sured, patients tend to stay away. Other doctors get wary, too—they hesitate to work in association with a physician who may implicate them in malpractice actions and be unable to pay for the consequences.

But won't plaintiff's lawyers drop a malpractice case once they find a doctor is uninsured? "Anyone who believes that can wake up and find he's been kicked in the assets," says Alfred S. Julien, a nationally known attorney who practices in New York City. "Most doctors are in a high-income bracket, they've accumulated property and money, and a good lawyer knows how to go after it to satisfy a judgment."

The whole situation is summed up by Florida malpractice defense attorney Frederick E. Hasty III. When asked by a doctor whether it's safe to go bare, he replied, "If you like skydiving, skating on thin ice, and riding the rapids in an old inner tube, then going bare is for you."

Whether you're insured or not, there are ways to identify suit-prone patients. Find out how in the next chapter.

7

Spotting patients likely to sue

The warning signs are there. When they start flashing, watch out.

The woman was attractive, articulate, and well groomed. "I understand you're the very best in your field," she told the doctor on their first meeting, "and that's fine. I want the best, and I need the best."

On subsequent visits, she was lavish in her praise of the doctor's efforts to treat her. The trouble was, she complained of "fatigue, nervousness, and aches and pains all over"—a vague problem that the doctor was never able to resolve to the woman's satisfaction.

Even then, she assured the doctor, "I'm not angry at you— I'm sure you did your very best. It's just not good enough."

A month later, she filed a malpractice suit against the doctor. It was a meritless case and was subsequently dismissed. Nevertheless, it caused the doctor to suffer considerable strain and inconvenience.

Another doctor, who's had plenty of experience with this

"flattering" type of patient, comments, "I call them gunny-sackers. They collect and suppress resentments, overcompensate for them, then explode all over you in a flash of anger. The best way to handle them is to cool their overenthusiasm at the start. Make it clear that you're not a miracle worker and that they're not to expect miracles."

Of course, there's no sure-fire way to identify patients who are going to sue you, but surveys and studies have pinpointed characteristics that should put you on guard. Here are the most common.

The complainers

These are the exact opposite of the flatterers. They find fault with everything from their neighbors to the space program. And chances are, sooner or later, they're going to find fault with you. A typical example:

The first time this patient, a bus driver, came to the doctor, he blamed his chronic headaches on his neighbors. According to him, they were deadbeats, hell-raisers, perverts, and of highly suspect legitimacy. Then on subsequent visits, he railed bitterly on the pope, the president of the United States, the local garbage-collection service, and the poor quality of tomatoes today.

Finally, the patient got around to criticizing the treatment he was receiving. He became so hostile that the doctor, wisely, referred him to a medical center "where they have facilities to deal with your special problem."

The complainer you should particularly look out for is the one who bad-mouths doctors he's seen before coming to you. He may be trying to find ammunition for a suit against a doctor who's offended him, or he may be trying to set you up for a legal potshot.

In any event, don't say anything that might be construed as criticism of another doctor, treat the patient conservatively, and if he doesn't follow your clinical advice, suggest he find a doctor whose opinions he can respect.

Also within this category is the doctor-shopper. Medically, he doesn't know what he wants, or he instinctively dislikes what he gets, or both. Treat him cautiously, too.

The experts

A physician I know was once amused by a woman patient who jotted down everything he said and did in her own little notebook. He was less amused when the patient later used her notes to back up a malpractice suit. The doctor's treatment, she charged, ran counter to articles she had read in a variety of women's magazines—a complaint that was ultimately thrown out of court.

Be especially wary when this consumerist type of patient tries to get a guarantee of cure out of you. Once you make such a guarantee, of course, and you can't pay off on it, you're in a risky area.

A doctor in one survey tells how to deal with this sort of patient: "Try never to get cornered into saying a certain sequence of symptoms makes you suspect 'X' diagnosis. And do your best to get the whole history at once, since I've found a lot of these patients just dole out bits and pieces at a time."

The malingerers

An exasperated woman practically dragged her husband into a doctor's office and declared, "He's not a mule, but you'll probably have to hit him over the head with a club to get him to pay attention!"

The doctor soon learned what the wife was talking about. The patient missed appointments, didn't take medications prescribed for him, made a lot of silly excuses for not complying with instructions, and generally resisted treatment.

This sort of patient falls into two groups—those who don't care what happens to them, or those who expect the doctor to cure them without any effort on their part. Either way, they can spell legal trouble.

Safeguard yourself with meticulous records, making specific notes on appointments not kept, instructions not complied with, prescriptions not filled, or medications not taken.

It's also advisable to have a member of your staff present, or a member of the patient's family, when you give a particularly important instruction. That way, the patient can't say he didn't receive the instruction, or that he doesn't remember your giving it—two favorite excuses.

The cynics

He seemed to be a jolly fellow, full of wisecracks, even though he had a history of heart disease. "Tell me," he said on first meeting a new cardiologist, "Have you fellows cured the common cold yet?"

The doctor laughed. A year later, he was less mirthful when the jolly fellow filed a malpractice suit against him. The doctor's first reaction was, "I can't believe it. He's such a good-natured guy."

Just because a patient cracks jokes doesn't necessarily mean he's good-natured. If the jokes are cynical, they may be masking a deep-felt resentment against the medical condition and an antagonism toward doctors he feels aren't dealing with it properly.

So be sure the joke isn't on you when a patient consistently makes cracks like, "Bury any mistakes today, Doc?"..."How's your golf game?"..."Forget the medical advice—how about some investment tips"..."Do I really need this checkup, Doc, or do you need the check?"

You just might be talking to a patient who has a disdain of the medical profession, or is highly skeptical about what it can accomplish.

The grievers

People who walk into a doctor's office aren't usually happy about being there, but some are gloomy for reasons other than ill health. An illustration:

The patient was a business executive who suffered from ulcers and hypertension. In giving his history, he mentioned that he had recently lost his high-paying job. He was also in financial difficulties. Therefore, the doctor made allowances about the patient's continuing dejection and tried to cheer him up whenever possible.

The patient reacted bitterly. On meeting the doctor in the parking lot one day, he observed, "I see you have a new Cadillac. Mine is getting old, but that doesn't matter—the finance company will be around for it any day now."

Another time, after disagreeing with the doctor on a minor point of treatment, he declared, "I just hope you're properly insured."

Forewarned, the doctor did what every physician should do when he feels he's dealing with a suit-prone patient: He closely checked his records to make sure they were comprehensive and well documented.

That didn't forestall a suit by the patient in this particular instance, but it did put the doctor in such a strong position that the plaintiff's lawyer quickly dropped the suit.

It's not enough for a doctor to spot suit-prone patients, however—he should also know how to handle patients' families. We'll go into that next.

8

A *patient's family ties can rope you into a lawsuit*

In concentrating on the patient's medical needs, you just might overlook the emotional needs of the family.

It started as a faulty medical diagnosis and ended as a landmark legal decision that broadens a physician's responsibility to close relatives of patients.

In handing down the decision, the California Supreme Court declared that a man who had suffered emotionally as a result of his ex-wife's medical care could sue separately for malpractice—even though the woman herself had not been injured physically. "Emotional injury," the court stated, "may be as severe and debilitating as physical harm, and is no less deserving of redress."

The facts of the case: The patient was an attractive young wife and mother who went to a South San Francisco hospital for a routine multiphasic physical examination. After the examination, a staff doctor told the patient she had syphilis. He also urged her to inform her husband, so he could undergo treatment. Tests, however, showed that the husband did not have syphilis.

The emotional impact on both the wife and the husband was shattering, and they eventually divorced.

Meanwhile, the wife underwent treatment for syphilis, including massive doses of penicillin. In addition, she feared that her only child, a young girl, might somehow contract the disease.

Then it was discovered that the diagnosis had been wrong—she did not have syphilis. Outraged, the woman filed a malpractice suit against the hospital and the doctor who had made the diagnosis.

Her ex-husband then consulted a lawyer to find out if he could successfully press a separate malpractice suit on the grounds of emotional distress. There didn't seem to be much chance, especially as the couple had divorced. As legal precedent stood at that time, courts were more concerned with tangible evidence, such as physical damage, than with emotional intangibles.

Nevertheless, the lawyer filed a complaint that stated the husband had been deprived of his wife's "love, companionship, affection, society, sexual relations, solace, support, and services" because of the inaccurate diagnosis.

After a costly legal battle that dragged on for years, the case wound up in the state supreme court, which ruled in favor of the husband.

The decision not only broadens a doctor's responsibility to close relatives of a patient—it places emotional harm on a par with physical injury as a cause of action. In short, doctors would be well advised to keep in mind the effects that treatment might have on the patient and on the family.

Here are other ways that repercussions from a family could lead to litigation.

Lack of communication

In many cases, this is simply lack of understanding and consideration on the part of the doctor. Examples:

• A middle-aged woman was hospitalized for orthopedic surgery. It was an intricate, time-consuming procedure, and the patient's husband and two grown sons waited anxiously in the hospital lobby. Hours passed, and the family noticed other surgeons, still in their operating gowns, as they came down to report to the families of patients.

Finally the husband checked at the desk and found that his wife was in the recovery room. The surgeon had long since left the hospital. As he explained later, "I had to get back to the office. The operation had worked out well, and I didn't feel I had to hang around and talk about it."

The family felt differently. When the outcome of the operation turned out to be less than perfect, they prompted the patient to sue for malpractice.

• A man with a history of heart problems was rushed by ambulance to a hospital after he suffered a severe seizure. His adult son and daughter followed the ambulance by car. They watched nervously as the patient was admitted from the emergency room to the intensive care unit.

A couple of hours later, when the son and daughter went up to the ICU for a brief visit, the patient was nowhere to be found. In their highly charged emotional state, the children thought their father had died, and the daughter collapsed.

Later it was learned that the patient had simply been transferred to the coronary care unit. The cardiologist and internist who attended the patient had left the hospital without notifying the children of the transfer.

Ultimately, the patient returned home in stable condition, though subject for a while to anginal pain. The family seized on that—and the fact that no medication had been prescribed to relieve the pain—to bring a malpractice charge against the two attending physicians and the hospital.

Moral: If a patient is weighing the possibility of a malpractice suit, a doctor's indifference to the family in their time of stress can be a deciding factor.

Insufficient explanation

Most physicians explain the procedures they recommend to patients and their families, but sometimes the explanations don't go far enough.

One surgeon, for example, informed a patient's husband that she was being hospitalized for surgical investigation of lumps in her breast. After the biopsy, which showed the lumps to be malignant, the doctor did a radical bilateral mastectomy without further consulting the husband.

The surgeon's only explanation to the shocked husband was, "The patient was already anesthetized, the operation had to be performed, and I went ahead and did it."

The husband didn't accept the contention that radical surgery "had to be performed," and he and his wife sued the surgeon for malpractice. The suit probably would have been averted if the surgeon had explained contingencies that could arise during the procedure and what he might have to do to deal with them.

In another case, a surgeon performed a thyroidectomy on a married businesswoman, then went on to several other operations he had scheduled. Meanwhile, the businesswoman's husband was frantically waiting in the hospital lobby. He remembered that long wait, and when his wife suffered side effects from the operation, he encouraged her to sue the doctor.

Now when that doctor has back-to-back surgeries, he's very careful to explain the situation in advance to families. As soon as each operation is concluded, he sends an assistant to report to the family. Later he comes down to speak personally with the family and answer any questions they might have.

What else can doctors do to keep families informed? Four practical tips:

1. Have the patient designate a family representative to whom you'll report anything you might have to say about the

case. This will get assorted cousins and aunts off your back and telephone.

2. Explain to the family representative what has transpired and what the patient's prospects are. Be careful not to be over-optimistic—that might be misinterpreted as a guarantee of a cure. If all is not well, be honest but not blunt or brutal.

3. If a serious medical situation arises, include a close relative in a pre-treatment consultation with the patient. This will prevent misunderstanding by the family of what you propose to do and why you're doing it.

4. Be especially scrupulous in your explanation if the patient is a child, particularly a young athlete or a budding ballet star. One couple sued a doctor for malpractice because their Little Leaguer lost three days of practice.

Doctors, of course, are not always to blame when families get litigation-minded. Some family members may be set for a fight as soon as they see you. Beware of the following warning signals.

• They question you closely and make it plain they're consumer-minded. As consumerists, they may instinctively regard you as an enemy. Don't give them any ammunition for a legal battle. If their anti-doctor remarks are too antagonistic, offer to refer the patient to another doctor.

• They seem doubtful about your proposed treatment. Explain that treatment in detail, and ask the patient if he has any objections. If he does, suggest he try another physician.

• They're bearing heavy personal burdens, such as feelings of guilt about a terminally ill relative, or one who's been badly hurt in an accident. This sort of guilt almost always stems from past neglect of the relative, usually one who's elderly. If the patient dies, that self-loathing by family members just might turn into hostility toward you. Don't give them any grounds for making a legal issue out of it.

There's another type of family you should beware of—your own office family. We'll look into that next.

9

*I*s your staff leading you into legal hot water?

In the eyes of the law, the best doctor in the world is only as good as his worst employee.

A woman once came to me with a complaint that she'd been incorrectly treated by a "dumb doctor."

"How do you know he's dumb?" I asked her.

"Because everybody who works for him is dumb."

It's common for patients to relate a doctor to his staff. Therefore, quite often, patient dissatisfaction with an office assistant will put the doctor on a malpractice spot.

As an employer, you're legally responsible in most jurisdictions for the acts of staff members within the scope of their jobs. Consequently, it's advisable to take a close look periodically at your office environment and staff conduct, with an eye to discovering areas of potential patient discontent. Here are questions to ask yourself:

What sort of reception do patients receive?

The telephone is usually a patient's first point of contact with
your office. What happens then can badly affect the patient's
impression of you and your practice. If the receptionist is
abrupt, indifferent, rude, arrogant, or ignorant, that patient
will come to you—if he or she comes at all—in a negative or
hostile mood.

Let's take an actual case. A wealthy married woman moved
to a new neighborhood and called the office of an internist to
whom she'd been referred.

"I'd like to make an appointment to talk to the doctor," she
told the receptionist.

"Talk about what?"

"Oh, general matters—just to get acquainted."

"Doctor doesn't make appointments like that—he's very
busy. Isn't there anything wrong with you?"

"Well, I have hypertension. I could come in for a blood-
pressure test."

"You'll have to fast for that."

"I don't think you understand. I don't mean a blood test
where you have to fast. I mean a blood-*pressure* test."

"Don't tell me I don't understand—this is a medical office
and I work here."

The woman persisted, and finally got an appointment.
When she arrived at the office, the receptionist was sitting
behind a closed, frosted glass partition. The woman had to rap
on it several times before the receptionist slid the partition
open and snapped, "Take a seat. I'll call you."

There were other patients in the waiting room, and the
woman felt a combination of embarrassment and anger as she
sat down. Later, after filling out a history form, she was led by
another assistant to an examination room.

"Take off your coat and blouse," the assistant said, then left
without further explanation.

The woman sat in the chilly cubicle for almost half an hour.
Fuming, she was on the verge of leaving when the doctor

finally rushed in, explained he'd been busy, and apologized for the delay.

"Couldn't one of your staff have informed me of that?" the woman asked.

"Didn't they?"

"No."

"I'm sorry. I guess they're busy, too."

That appeased the woman, but only for the moment. She still felt resentful whenever she returned to that office.

"It was like prodding an aching tooth," she later told me. "I didn't like going there, and I suppose I shouldn't have gone at all. I guess I was just looking for a chance to get even with those bitchy assistants."

Her chance came when the doctor made a mistake in her treatment, and she sued him for malpractice. That was her way of getting even with those "bitchy assistants."

How can you ensure that your office staff will make patients feel welcome?

Here are some tips I've gleaned from some professional office management consultants.

• Phone your own office from time to time unexpectedly. Is the tone of your receptionist warm and encouraging, or cold and forbidding? Does she bark, "Hold on" without explanation, or does she say, "I'm busy on another line, but I'll get right back to you. Please hold"?

If you have any doubt at all, bring up the matter of phone etiquette at a staff meeting, and emphasize the importance of first impressions on a patient.

Also stress the importance of dealing courteously with all your patients. I know of one elderly gentlemen who sued for malpractice after he fell off an examination table. The suit was triggered by a young assistant who quipped to the patient as she was helping him onto the table, "Up you go, Pop!"

Most mature patients don't like being treated in a flippant manner. They want to be treated with decency and respect.

• We all walk into restaurants and see the sign, "Wait Here To Be Seated." If you wait too long without anyone coming forward, you feel uncomfortable or annoyed, especially if any diners are gawking at you. You might even walk out.

There may be times when a patient feels like walking out of your waiting room. Avert that by training your assistants to greet patients as soon as they come in. "May I help you?" is a good opening. Or, if the assistant is momentarily busy, "I'll be right with you."

Patients who wait to see a doctor, of course, are often anxious and apprehensive—feelings that can be exacerbated if the wait goes on too long. If you're running late or have been thrown off schedule by an emergency, have one of your assistants explain to waiting patients what's happening, apologize, and offer to reschedule appointments. Thoughtfulness such as that has averted more than a few malpractice suits.

• Patients are sometimes reluctant to complain to a doctor, but they'll open up to an assistant. Instruct your staff to report to you immediately if a patient grumbles or gripes to them, no matter how trivial it may seem. A minor squawk just might develop into a full-voiced malpractice claim. By catching it early, you'll have a chance to clear up the matter through an honest interchange with the patient.

• From time to time, when you're chatting with a patient, ask how he or she feels about your employees. Are they polite, efficient, and understanding? Can improvements be made?

The overall aim is to make patients feel wanted, not rejected. That's not only a safeguard against a malpractice complaint—it's good patient care.

Are your employees playing doctor?

After office staff members have been around a physician for a while, they pick up quite a bit of medical knowledge. That's fine, if they use it discreetly and constructively, but it can be catastrophic if they overstep themselves. Examples:

• A patient phoned her doctor's office when he happened to be away.

"Damn!" the patient said. "My three-year-old is feeling sick, and I just don't know what to do."

"Well, that sounds like the flu that's going around," the receptionist declared, offering instant diagnosis. "If I were you, I'd give her aspirin and fluids. That's what the doctor has been prescribing."

Two days later, the child was rushed to a hospital, where she died of meningitis. The mother sued both the doctor and the receptionist for malpractice, a case that was settled out of court for $500,000.

• A woman dropped by her doctor's office while he was on hospital rounds. She spoke to the office nurse about a urinary tract infection that had reoccurred.

"Should I take the same antibiotic the doctor previously prescribed?" she asked the nurse.

"Sure," the nurse said, "I think that would be all right."

It wasn't all right. The woman was pregnant, and her baby died of complications caused by the antibiotic.

The doctor settled a subsequent malpractice suit for the limit of his coverage.

• A middle-aged man was worried after a consultation with a surgeon.

"Looks like I'll have to have a heart bypass," the patient remarked to the assistant at the front desk.

"Don't worry," she assured him. "Doctor is very good at that procedure—you won't have any trouble. I can promise you that."

The operation was prolonged by unexpected complications, and the patient died several weeks later. His family successfully sued the surgeon on the grounds that his assistant had made a promise that amounted to a warranty.

The crucial point of all this is that only a licensed physician can diagnose illnesses and treat patients. Impress this on your staff, point out that even well-intentioned remarks can be construed as medical advice, and instruct them not to volunteer medical opinions.

Moreover, if you're away from the office, make sure that the staff refers all medical questions from patients to the doctor who's covering for you. Also leave clear rules on how assistants should deal with inquiries about prescription refills and other routine matters.

At all times, stress that employees should never, never make any remarks to a patient that could be interpreted as a guarantee of a cure.

Are you delegating too much?

There are some clinical chores that paramedical personnel can do as well as you can—maybe better. Consequently, in the interest of efficiency, it makes sense to delegate those tasks. But how far can you go? When does delegation become risky, even reckless? Consider the following cases.

• An internist routinely had his nurse pass along treatment instructions to patients by phone. On one occasion, a patient called back to report side effects from a prescribed drug. After checking the medical record, the nurse told the patient to stay on the medication because "that's what the doctor ordered. Give it a chance."

Subsequently the side effects grew worse, and the patient was hospitalized. Later, she sued the doctor for malpractice. On the advice of his insurance carrier, he settled out of court. The case would have been a difficult one to defend, the carrier felt, because the nurse had gone beyond her delegated duties and had not consulted the doctor about that patient's inquiry.

• An RN, on instruction from her doctor-employer, gave non-narcotic injections. One patient collapsed after an injection and had to be revived by the doctor. The patient then sued him, charging that he had negligently allowed the nurse to give injections.

The suit was dropped after the doctor presented a perfect,

six-point defense: (1) The nurse was well trained in giving injections. (2) She did not exceed the doctor's orders. (3) Her duties fell within the state's legal code. (4) They were clearly defined. (5) The doctor supervised her work. (6) He was on hand to give back-up care if needed.

Those points pretty well cover what you should do when delegating medical tasks to assistants. It's also wise to consult a knowledgeable local lawyer on the delegation laws in your particular state. They vary somewhat around the country.

Is patient confidentiality protected?

The receptionist and a patient were chatting at the front desk. They knew each other well, and the patient confided, "I'm thinking of having my breasts enlarged, but I just don't know. I'm nervous when it comes to surgery."

"Listen," said the receptionist, "check with your friend, Mrs. Brown. She's had that operation."

"You're kidding!"

"No. Ask her."

The patient did just that the next time she met Mrs. Brown, who was less than pleased by the inquiry.

"How do you know I had that operation?" she demanded.

"We have the same doctor. His receptionist mentioned it to me when I told her I was nervous about surgery."

Outraged, Mrs. Brown retained a lawyer to sue the doctor and the receptionist for invasion of privacy. The suit was later dropped, but not before the doctor suffered through some worrisome days.

Careless comments by office assistants lead to lawsuits quite often, and even an innocuous remark can be interpreted as a breach of confidentiality. Emphasize periodically to your staff that patients' privacy must be protected, especially on such sensitive matters as pregnancy, abortion, birth control, venereal disease, emotional problems, and finances.

Furthermore, information about a patient should never be given to another person by telephone unless the identity of the caller can be verified. Before details of any medical treatment are disclosed, authorization from the patient should be obtained, preferably in writing. Keep in mind this comment by David Karp, a California malpractice claims-prevention specialist: "A good staff can go a long way toward holding down a doctor's litigation risks."

Discretion in your association with other doctors will also hold down those risks. We'll take that up in the next chapter.

10

Guilt by association

Whether you practice alone or in a group, you can be held liable for the acts of other doctors—in ways that may surprise you.

On a recent occasion after I'd spoken at a medical meeting, I sat around with some physicians, discussing the legal aspects of doctoring. An interesting topic came up: Who bears the heaviest liability, the soloist or the doctor who is part of a group or partnership?

One soloist said, "I feel I'm better off alone. I'm not responsible for the acts of guys I just happen to be associated with."

I asked him a series of questions. Did other doctors ever cover for him? Did he make referrals? Did he call in consultants? Did he ever work as part of a team with other physicians in the care of a patient?

The answers were all Yes.

"Then you bear just as much responsibility as a doctor in a group," I told the soloist. "Strictly speaking, there are no soloists in practice today. They all have to depend professionally on other doctors, and there's always a liability attached."

To illustrate my point, I cited the following two cases:

1. An internist referred a patient to a surgeon, who botched the operation. The internist was named along with the surgeon in a malpractice suit, and both had to pay substantial damages. The internist lost because he hadn't properly checked the competence of the surgeon, who had a history of complaints against him.

2. A GP went on vacation and left his patients in the care of a young FP who was new in town and, as it was later stated, "needed the work." He apparently also needed more experience. One of the patients suffered severe side effects from a wrongly prescribed drug, and both physicians were hit for damages.

Moral: Make a reasonable effort to ascertain the competence of any doctor you call on to treat, or even examine, any of your patients.

Physicians in a partnership or group, of course, have long been looked on as liable in some circumstances for acts of associates. Now the Uniform Partnership Act has been interpreted so widely in one state that it may adversely affect doctors all over the country.

The facts of the case: In 1959, a Massachusetts surgeon operated on an auto mechanic for carcinoma of the rectum. Although the patient's recovery from the surgery was recorded as uneventful, he suffered various complications, including draining from the operation site, foul odor, and difficulty in walking. In 1978, three years after the original surgeon had died, another surgeon explored the patient's perineal sinus and removed a Penrose drain.

That's when the patient decided he was entitled to damages. The question was: Whom should he sue? The surgeon who had originally operated had long since died, and the surgery dated all the way back to 1959.

The patient and his lawyer finally zeroed in on nine physicians who were believed to have been partners in the same practice as the operating surgeon. A malpractice suit was filed in 1980.

The question now was: Did a partnership exist when the operation took place?

Five of the accused doctors had in fact been associated with the surgeon, but they contended they had been employees, not partners. In 1962, the multispecialty group had become a clinic under another name. That's when the five accused doctors were told they were junior partners. They contended that was simply a title, since they were on salary.

Also around 1962, the four other defendants joined the clinic as junior partners. Later, a professional corporation was formed. Subsequently, the shareholder doctors split up and formed several other practices.

This was the complex, baffling case that went all the way up to the Supreme Judicial Court of Massachusetts. A decision, handed down in 1983, concluded that all nine defendants had at one time or another been in the same partnership. Therefore, it was ruled, they were liable under the state's Uniform Partnership Act—which gave the judgment wide application. All but two states—Georgia and Louisiana—have similar laws.

The plaintiff and his wife were ultimately awarded a total of $500,000—even though the defendants had never known the patient.

After the verdict, the plaintiff's attorney made a comment that's pertinent to all practicing physicians: "When you join a partnership, keep in mind that under the Uniform Partnership Act, you're responsible for any previous act of negligence that the partnership is responsible for, up to the limit of the partnership assets. Your personal assets are protected by the law, but you risk having the partnership liquidated to pay for the malpractice of a doctor you may have never met."

Another root cause of malpractice suits is common lack of communication among doctors and other medical personnel working on a case. Example:

In a case recently filed, a young mother was hospitalized with an inflamed gallbladder and probable pancreatitis. Three days before a gallbladder operation was scheduled, the patient's family physician was requested by the surgeon to have a workup done. The FP complied, but neglected to do electrolyte studies. Moreover, he didn't order an electrocardiogram until the night before the operation.

By the time of surgery, a "take it for granted" syndrome had set in. The surgeon figured all tests were OK because the FP hadn't informed him differently. The FP thought the surgeon would check out test findings. The anesthesiologist didn't even ask about the tests. And no one in the X-ray department passed along results of the ECG to the doctors in the case.

The patient went into cardiopulmonary arrest right after the operation and died. Because of lack of communication, not one of the doctors involved knew that the ECG reading was abnormal. All were named in the suit, along with the hospital.

Moral: Never take for granted that someone else on a treatment team has performed a vital function. Check it out—make sure it's been done.

In cases of this sort, where there are multiple defendants, I've noticed an increasing tendency of defense attorneys to put pressure on a doctor to join in a general settlement, even though he feels he's done no wrong.

That happened in a case where an OBG, two pediatricians, a nurse midwife, and a hospital were charged with negligence in the care of a newborn who suffered brain damage. After the pediatricians settled out of court for the basic limits of their malpractice insurance policies, the OBG said that he "felt pressure" from his own insurance carrier to do the same. He wanted to fight the case but he gave in because he thought the carrier would "get even." The total settlement: $2.3 million.

Are doctors entirely at the mercy of lawyers in this kind of "shotgun" case, where charges are fired at everyone in sight? No. A physician who's convinced he's been dragged into a suit without justification has recourse to the law. For example: A doctor was named in a suit mainly because the plaintiff's lawyer wanted his deposition for use against the principal defendant. The doctor was subsequently dropped from the suit, but not before he had suffered considerable worry and disruption of his practice. He countersued the plaintiff's lawyer, charging him with improper motives, and won a jury award of $175,000 in general and punitive damages.

More about countersuits later. Right now, in the next chapter, we'll take a look at how hospitals can suck you into a malpractice suit.

11

*I*s your hospital a liability trap?

Many hospitals today compete rather than cooperate with doctors. Here are the danger areas.

Hospitals used to be called physicians' workshops. Everybody involved worked toward a common goal—the best possible patient care.

Today, that cooperation has largely turned to competition. Economically and professionally, what the hospital wants isn't always what physicians want—or, at least, should want in their own best legal interest. Cost-containment pressures to get a patient out of a hospital as fast as possible, for example, can explode into a malpractice suit against a doctor who's accused of providing less than proper care.

There are many other examples of how this ever-developing adversary relationship increases the professional liability of physicians. I've divided them into four categories: Hospital policy, hospital conditions, hospital nurses, and divide-and-conquer tactics. Let's take a closer look at those categories.

Hospital policy

One Sunday morning in February 1975, a 4-year-old boy was brought to a hospital emergency room obviously suffering great pain and distress. He also showed other symptoms of serious illness. Nevertheless, because the mother hadn't brought proof of insurance coverage, the boy was refused admission for inpatient care. He died in another hospital less than a week later.

I represented the parents in a wrongful-death action against the first hospital and the child's attending physician. That doctor, by all indications a decent man and a dedicated practitioner, was drawn into the case largely because of the hospital's policy of denying admission to patients who couldn't prove they could pay.

Doctors can easily stray into this sort of liability trap, especially as hospitals try to exert more and more control over their medical staffs. Hospital conditions that cause legal problems for attending doctors can usually be seen. Troublesome hospital policies, on the other hand, can be much harder to detect.

And even when poor policies are easy to see, doctors may be so financially tied to the hospital that they look the other way. Consequently, when plaintiff's attorneys strike, physicians are targets as well as the hospital. That 1975 incident shows all too well what can happen.

On February 13 of that year, Sherry Bland took her 4-year-old son, Michael, to the office of a family physician in California. The boy had a temperature of 101 and seemed to be suffering from an upper respiratory tract infection. The FP prescribed erythromycin and Phenergan.

For the following week, Michael appeared to improve. Then, at 6:30 a.m. on February 23, a Sunday, the boy's bizarre behavior woke up his parents. He was delirious and had a high fever. His father, Joseph, called the emergency room at a nearby hospital. A nurse said to bathe the boy in tepid water, then bring him to the ER. Mrs. Bland bathed her son for about 20 minutes, then drove him to the hospital, arriving about 8 a.m.

After a 45-minute wait, the doctor on duty in the ER ordered a CBC and chest x-rays and used a Q-tip to remove a greenish fluid that had started oozing from Michael's ears. He registered a temperature of 103.

By coincidence, the FP was making rounds at the hospital that morning. When he learned that Michael was in the ER, he went there and conferred with the doctor on duty. They decided that the boy was seriously ill and probably should be admitted for inpatient treatment.

The FP then called the admitting clerk and said that he and the ER physician wanted the child hospitalized. (Keep in mind that word "wanted"—it proved to be critical.) The clerk asked if Mrs. Bland had proof of insurance coverage. The FP, who knew that she was a Medi-Cal (California's version of Medicaid) patient, asked if she had her card with her. She said No, it was at home.

The clerk then said that unless the FP could declare that an emergency existed, the child could not be admitted. Under state hospital regulations, as the FP understood them, an emergency existed only if the situation was life-threatening. Neither the FP nor the ER physician, both of whom had diagnosed the boy's illness as otitis media, felt that his life was in immediate danger.

Consequently, he was denied admission. After receiving a shot of penicillin I.M., Michael went home with his mother around noon.

His temperature continued to rise, and he broke out in red blotches all over his body. At 2:45 p.m., while resting in his mother's arms, Michael lapsed into a coma. Mrs. Bland rushed him to the local fire station. From there, he was taken by ambulance to another hospital in the area, where he arrived at 3 p.m.

The ER doctor did a spinal tap and determined that the boy had spinal meningitis and encephalitis. He was admitted for treatment immediately. On March 1, six days after he was turned away at the original hospital, Michael Bland died.

Later, the parents contacted my associate in San Diego, John N. Learnard, who has special expertise in medico-legal matters. He and I divided up the workload. John would take care of the documentation, investigation, and interrogatories, and I would handle the trial arguments. We then filed suit against the FP and the hospital where Michael had been refused admission. The hospital is a private, for-profit facility.

We studied the hospital's policies on admission and credit and found numerous instances in which personnel were ordered to determine patients' financial status before admitting them, and to insist on proof of insurance coverage or sufficient cash resources.

In a deposition, the man who had been administrator of the hospital when Michael was turned away reinforced our finding. The hospital did not have to accept anyone who lacked sufficient money or insurance, he said.

Could Mrs. Bland have made a cash guarantee, possibly through a relative? The former administrator replied that very often Medi-Cal families "are the kind that do not have well-to-do relatives who can pay for them."

That raised the possibility that Michael was refused admission simply *because* his mother was on Medi-Cal. Making a profit is fine, but I felt this was a classic case of putting money ahead of medical need.

Were physicians at the hospital aware of the admission policy? It seemed to be common knowledge. We found members of the medical and nursing staffs who said they'd testify that seriously ill patients had been rejected because they couldn't guarantee payment. One ER physician cited several instances in which patients, including some who were dying, had to be sent to other hospitals because they couldn't meet the financial criteria for admission.

Yet, as far as we could discover, no member of the medical

staff had ever made a formal complaint to the hospital administration about this policy.

In any event, rejection had been the last thing the Blands expected at the hospital. At the time, they were a struggling young couple. He was out of work and doing odd jobs to make ends meet. Michael, the eldest of their three children, had suffered from various minor illnesses since birth.

The family was a typical one in the FP's practice. He had a heavy load of low-income patients in a blue-collar area. There was a real medical need there, and the FP did his best to fill it.

Nevertheless, I was disturbed by his behavior in the hospital ER. He first determined that Michael was seriously ill, but then decided that a life-threatening emergency did not exist.

It seemed to me that the FP had been more worried about hospital red tape than the well-being of his patient. That's why we included him in the suit. As more facts came to light, however, I had second thoughts.

• Mrs. Bland told us that the FP had been upset by the hospital's refusal to admit Michael and had made her promise to bring the child to his office early the next morning. When they didn't show up, he called to find out what had happened. By then, of course, Michael had been admitted to the other hospital.

• The FP stated he did not know that Michael had vomited in the ER reception room after being denied admission, though there was some dispute about whether the nurse had reported this to him. If it had been reported, he later insisted, he would have declared that a life-threatening emergency existed and would have had the boy admitted.

If Michael had been admitted, the FP stated in a deposition, "I would have prescribed 600,000 units of penicillin every six hours, all intravenously, for his otitis media. And dextrose 5 percent with water, 50cc per hour, would have been prescribed for dehydration, along with aspirin for his fever."

The FP added that if any symptoms of meningitis had appeared, he'd have increased the I.V. dosage of penicillin to 1 million units every four hours and performed a spinal tap.

Our medical experts advised us that if the FP's course of inpatient treatment had been carried out, the child's life probably would have been saved.

At that point, John Learnard and I decided to settle with the FP's insurance carrier.

The real root of any mistake he might have made, it seemed to us, was in allowing himself to become too closely tied to the hospital. He rented office space nearby, and he needed hospital facilities for his work. Perhaps that made it difficult for him to challenge hospital policy.

We agreed to a token settlement of $2,900, with the understanding that the FP would be available for testimony in court.

The trial began in February 1981. There had been considerable publicity about the case, and the courtroom was packed.

At the request of hospital attorneys, the judge quickly blocked us on two important fronts: (1) We weren't permitted to plead for punitive damages. (2) We weren't allowed to present testimony that the hospital had pursued its discriminatory admission policy prior to the Bland case. The judge ruled such testimony would be inflammatory.

The defendants contended that the hospital had no duty to admit patients to the hospital just because they were treated in the ER. That, I said, was like treating a badly wounded man with a Band-Aid in the ER, then sending him into the parking lot to bleed to death. I argued further that any hospital soliciting patients by way of an ER sign had a duty to follow up with care as requested by treating physicians.

Then came a tussle over whether the FP and the ER physician had "wanted" or "ordered" the child to be admitted. If an order had been issued, the defendants claimed, Michael would have been admitted.

I pointed out that the FP had made it clear to the admitting clerk that the boy was seriously ill and should be hospitalized.

I added that if the FP had known about the child's vomiting in the reception room, he would have insisted on admitting him. The defense attorneys argued that the nurse had informed the FP about the vomiting, but she was never called as a witness.

The principal defense argument was that Michael was "doomed" and would have died no matter what had been done for him at the hospital. Their medical expert, a neurosurgeon, testified to that effect.

Our expert, a pediatric neurologist who'd had extensive experience with cases of spinal meningitis in children, testified that Michael would have had an 80 percent chance of survival if he'd been admitted and treated promptly.

When the FP testified, he refuted the defense contention that Michael had been denied admission for medical reasons. He said that, in his opinion, if Mrs. Bland had been able to show proof of valid insurance coverage, or had been able to produce sufficient funds, Michael would have been admitted when the FP made his request to the clerk.

After a three-week trial, the jury deliberated two and a half days—primarily to debate the amount of damages. The amount awarded to the Blands was $300,000—$250,000 for the wrongful death of Michael, and $50,000 to his mother for emotional distress.

At the time, it was the highest award ever returned in California for the wrongful death of a minor. If punitive damages had been allowed, it would have been much higher.

After the verdict, I understand that some members of the medical staff at the hospital pressed for policy changes. The point here, of course, is that the doctors should have moved much sooner than they did. When a hospital pursues a policy that interferes with proper patient care, doctors should complain in writing immediately to the chief of the medical staff. That serves two purposes. It puts doctors on record as being opposed to the policy, and it helps unite them in an effort to change it.

As the Bland case shows, a doctor who doesn't try to buck a bad system may end up its victim.

Hospital conditions

I'm not talking here about broken-down equipment or vomit on the floor. Rather, I'm trying to point out conditions that might be missed by a doctor—until a malpractice complaint brings them rudely to his attention.

In one very large, very efficient hospital, for example, an elderly spinster was scheduled for a gallbladder operation. When the surgeon dropped by the day before the operation, he found her so upset she couldn't stop crying. The operation had to be called off.

Later, the patient's relatives moved her to another hospital, where the operation was performed by a second surgeon. When complications followed, the relatives induced the patient to include the first hospital and the original surgeon in a malpractice suit. Because of them, the complaint stated, the elderly spinster had been forced by nurses to fill out a questionnaire about her sex life, her phobias, and the size of her bank account. This, the complaint added, was the cause of the patient's emotional distress, which in turn had led to the surgical complications.

The accused surgeon protested that he hadn't even known about the offensive hospital form. The plaintiff's attorney contended that he *should* have known about it.

The case was eventually dropped, but not before the surgeon himself sustained a lot of emotional distress. The offensive questionnaire disappeared from the hospital.

Of the many thousands of medical malpractice suits filed in the United States each year, about 80 percent stem from harm sustained by patients in hospitals. Most complaints name attending physicians along with the hospital, even though the doctors may be linked only indirectly to the alleged damage. Too many of those physicians, I've observed, either have blind spots when it comes to identifying liability traps in hospitals, or are reluctant to complain about them.

In a case in which a hospitalized patient was restless, the doctor ordered that bed rails be kept up. Later, he noticed that one bed rail was occasionally left down, but he did nothing about it.

Subsequently, the patient fell out of bed, broke her hip, and sued both the hospital and the doctor. In a deposition, the doctor denied responsibility on the ground that he had ordered the bed rails to be kept up. He admitted, however, that he had visited the patient on several occasions and saw that the bed rail was down.

"It's common in that place," he said, meaning the hospital. "They just don't pay attention to orders."

Nevertheless, even though he had issued a proper order, he hadn't followed up on it by bringing infractions to the attention of nurses or hospital authorities. The case was settled out of court—and the doctor's malpractice premium went up.

Infectious conditions in hospitals are another problem for attending physicians. Consider the following case:

A surgeon successfully performed an appendectomy, but the incision later became infected with staph, and a malpractice suit was filed. During the discovery process, it developed that four other patients in that operating ward had also suffered from staph. Previous acts of negligence aren't usually admissible in court. This time they were because they showed awareness of a dangerous condition.

Result: The plaintiff's attorney brought out the fact that the surgeon had known of the infectious condition and had done nothing about it. The case was settled.

Moral: If a physician knows, or should know, that a hospital infection is prevalent or probable, and does nothing about it, he's liable for damages.

Doctors can also slip up on conditions caused by a hospital's messy housekeeping. In one case, a patient recovering from back surgery was bothered by cleaners roughly moving his bed. He complained to his doctor, who said, "Sure, don't worry—I'll take care of it."

Several days later, the patient's back condition was severely aggravated when his bed was again jerked about by cleaners. He sued the hospital and the doctor for damages.

If the doctor had indeed passed on the patient's complaint to the housekeeping department, he probably would have been legally in the clear. As it turned out, however, he hadn't taken care of the matter, as he had promised the patient. The case was settled for $20,000, half of which was paid by the doctor.

Hospital nurses

Most hospital nurses do a great job under trying conditions. I applaud them, and I'm sure most physicians do, too. As in any other calling, though, some misfits get in. These present a particular peril for attending doctors. Several examples from hundreds I could cite:

• The patient was fitted with an indwelling Foley catheter. On several occasions he complained to his physician that he had been discomfited by an LPN when she was obtaining urine specimens. The physician requested the nurse to be more careful.

"Well, I'll try," she said, "but it's so awkward with that thing," meaning the Foley.

On the next occasion, in a desperate attempt to handle the catheter, she yanked it right out of the patient.

He suffered shock and a setback in treatment that required him to stay an extra two weeks in the hospital. He later sued the hospital and the attending physician for malpractice. On the recommendation of their insurance carriers, they agreed to settle out of court.

• A surgeon knew that a certain nurse was notoriously slow in answering patient call signals. Nevertheless, he continued to place patients under her care.

One of his patients, a policeman who'd been operated on for a gunshot wound, repeatedly pressed the nurse's call button late one night. She didn't respond, and the man bled to death. A resulting suit against the surgeon and the hospital was settled out of court. There was just no defense.

The main point to keep in mind: A physician who knows that a nurse is slipshod or incompetent, and allows her to attend to his patients, is liable for any resulting injury.

Don't figure it's all the hospital's responsibility.

Don't shrug it off and think, "Well, if I complain, I'll make enemies and risk losing my privileges."

Do complain. If hospital officials do nothing about it, put your complaint in writing and submit it to the appropriate medical staff committee. That way, you'll at least have some defense if you're ever hit with a case of this sort.

Another possible defense is contained in the "borrowed-servant" rule, which makes the doctor responsible for an assistant temporarily under his control, such as a hospital nurse. That rule, of course, can work against a doctor, but there are circumstances in which it could help him. A New Mexico case illustrates how that works:

An internist was called in to attend to a man who'd been brought to a hospital with chest pains. The doctor diagnosed myocardial infarction, and instructed the RN to administer 50mg of lidocaine hydrochloride. The nurse had some trouble with the vial, and the doctor—who was monitoring the patient—told her to get another one. Unfortunately, this vial contained far more of the drug than the discarded one, and the patient suffered irreversible brain damage.

The patient's widow then pressed a wrongful death action against the nurse and her employer, the hospital. The doctor, however, wasn't left off the hook—the hospital and the nurse filed a third-party suit against him, contending that he'd been in control of the nurse and should share some of the liability.

Prolonged and complex litigation followed, but the basic argument centered on the borrowed-servant doctrine. Had the internist been negligent in failing to discover and prevent the drug overdose? Had he been too busy in a life-and-death situation to check on the details of what the nurse was doing? Or had they both been negligent for failing to read the label of the second vial?

A jury decided in favor of the doctor, finding that only the hospital and the nurse had been negligent. The verdict was upheld by an appeals court. One judge wrote an opinion that is of particular interest to doctors:

"A judicial approach to the awesome responsibility of a physician must recognize that [his] primary duty in an emergency is to focus upon the serious medical problem from which a patient suffers. In such an emergency, the primary duty of the hospital is to focus upon the competence of nurses to perform their duties....

"The duty of the hospital should not be shifted to the doctor by way of the borrowed-servant doctrine unless the doctor selects the hospital nurse as an assistant due to his knowledge of her competence and exercises control and supervision over the details of her work, or unless [he] orders an assigned nurse to perform duties which [he] knows are beyond her level of competence...."

A comment by the doctor after the trial is also of interest: "One thing I learned from this experience is never to trust a nurse completely. In the future, I'll read medication labels myself—something doctors don't usually do."

I don't want to give the impression that a doctor should regard hospital nurses as enemies; they're among a doctor's greatest allies, and they should be valued as such.

Observes Donna Lee Guarriello, an RN who became a plaintiff's attorney in medical malpractice cases: "I've seen suits where, if a doctor had listened to a nurse instead of putting her down, he and his patient would have been the better for it. In one case, in which the physician ordered digitalis for a patient, the nurse observed and reported a definite deterioration. But the doctor pooh-poohed her fears and ordered the same dosage continued because the patient's symptoms didn't fit the classic description of digitalis toxicity.

"Over the weekend, the patient worsened and died. The nurse, who'd written her observations in the chart, was covered [as far as malpractice was concerned]. The doctor who'd dismissed them, wasn't."

An OBG confirms the importance of a mutually respectful doctor-nurse relationship: "A few years ago, a labor-room nurse's eloquent defense in my behalf blew a potential malpractice case to smithereens. The plaintiff's attorney admitted to me that, with the nurse on my side, there was no way he could win the case, and he dropped it.

"Learning to treat nurses as partners rather than pests can pay big dividends. The nurse's observations can carry tremendous weight in any case, for the obvious reason that she spends so much time with the patient as compared with the doctor. In or out of court, the hospital nurse who's taking care of your patient may be the best friend you've got."

Divide-and-conquer tactics

It's quite common for multiple defendants in a malpractice suit to point the finger of blame at each other. This especially happens when a hospital is involved and the defendants have separate malpractice insurance carriers.

In a classic case of this type, a hospital made a sliding-scale covenant with a plaintiff to limit its share of the total payment if a jury decided that malpractice had indeed occurred. Additionally, the hospital's attorney helped the plaintiff to place the burden of blame on the other defendant, an attending doctor. As a result, the doctor was hit with heavy damages.

When other doctors on the medical staff realized what had happened, they threatened to boycott the hospital and send their patients elsewhere. The rebellion subsided only after the hospital promised to be careful about making similar compacts in the future.

Along the same line comes this statement from a doctor that appeared in *Medical Economics* magazine: "My hospital is urging me to require patients to sign, as a condition of admission, an agreement that they won't sue for any complications of care. Is this sort of contract legal? If not, would it serve at least as a deterrent to malpractice suits?"

The answer from a panel of legal experts: "It wouldn't be

legally binding. While it might deter some patients from filing claims, it would also cause you trouble should you get sued. The plaintiff's lawyer could very well argue that you must have anticipated that you were going to bungle things."

In short, be cooperative in your dealings with your hospital, but be careful, too. Be equally careful when you're making a diagnosis. We'll take that up in the next chapter.

12

The dangers of diagnosis

Diagnostic errors head the malpractice list. That's scary, but it doesn't mean you should run scared.

According to a survey by a large professional liability insurer, one malpractice suit in four stems from the doctor's failure to correctly diagnose a patient's condition. That makes erroneous diagnosis the leading cause of malpractice complaints.

However, a doctor can misjudge a patient's condition and still not incur liability. The law recognizes that medicine is an inexact science, and courts have consistently ruled that mistakes in diagnosis must be considered in light of the way they're committed.

As an Illinois appellate court put it, "If the doctor has given the patient the benefit of his best judgment, assuming that judgment to be equal to that ordinarily used by reasonably well-qualified doctors in similar cases, he is not liable for negligence, even if that judgment is erroneous." For example:

A New York stockbroker collapsed at work, complaining of abdominal pain and symptoms of hyperventilation. He was rushed to a local hospital, where his personal physician made a diagnosis of gastroenteritis and decided that admission to the hospital wasn't necessary.

While the patient was walking to his car, though, he slumped to the pavement and died. In a subsequent malpractice suit, the doctor was accused of an error in diagnosis.

The case eventually went to an appellate court, which found that the doctor had reviewed the patient's history and hospital tests, checked him for signs of an aortic aneurysm, examined his heart by stethoscope, and searched for bile or blood in his vomitus. In addition, a medical examiner testified that the patient had been striken by a ventricular fibrillation without symptoms or warning.

Consequently, the court ruled that the doctor had exercised proper care in making his diagnosis and could not be held liable for the patient's death, which the court stated was "due to a tragic eventuality beyond the control of medicine today."

Now, I'm not trying to minimize the dangers of diagnosis. They're real and you should be aware of them. You should also be aware that there are precautions you can take to avert liability. Here they are:

Test wisely

In these days of cost containment, this is an area in which doctors are damned if they do and damned if they don't. The best thing to do is to follow advice contained in the AMA Principles of Medical Ethics: "While physicians should be conscious of costs and not provide or prescribe unnecessary services or ancillary facilities, social policy expects that concern for care the patient receives will be the physician's first consideration."

In short, never allow cost to override a decision on proper patient care, especially diagnosis.

According to a study by the Department of Health and Human Services, the majority of diagnostic errors are caused by inadequate examination and testing. This is confirmed by a claims executive with a doctor-owned malpractice insurance company, who says that failure to test is a bigger problem than misinterpretation of test results.

"We see it all the time," the executive adds. "A woman comes in complaining of a breast lump. On examination, the doctor determines that it's fibrocystic. He later does a mammogram that is negative. Then he stops. He doesn't do a biopsy, and the 'cyst' turns out to be a malignant neoplasm."

Part of the problem is that doctors frequently slip into a routine, or fall victim to overconfidence. They've seen the same symptoms thousands of times, and they assume a diagnosis without adequate testing. Just remember that "I took it for granted" is far from an adequate defense in court.

In addition to doing *enough* tests, doctors should do the *right* tests. This means testing intelligently. Know what standards are being followed in the profession. If the latest medical literature suggests that a particular test is indicated in a particular situation, perform it.

Similarly, if a specific complaint by the patient or your evaluation of symptoms indicates that lab work or X-rays are needed, get them. They'll not only help the patient—they'll help you if you should end up in court.

Examine thoroughly

In one case I'm familiar with, a patient complained of stomach pains, which he thought might be due to indigestion. The doctor, who was at the end of a hectic day, gave the patient a quick once-over and prescribed antacid tablets. Later, the patient's appendix ruptured.

Sued for malpractice due to misdiagnosis, the doctor's only excuse for the quick examination he'd given the patient was that he'd been busy and that the patient himself felt he only had indigestion. That, of course, was no defense at all. The case was settled out of court.

In another instance, a patient died after a physician misdiagnosed a strangulated intestine as a "virus." Commenting on the 10-minute examination the physician had given the patient, an appeals court declared, "Due care means more than a cursory examination. The fact that a condition is rare does not excuse failure to make inquiries."

If the patient is not capable of responding to inquiries, then members of the family should be questioned. Here are two examples of how that can work for or against the physician.

• When a father found his young son writhing in pain, he rushed the child to the family physician, who diagnosed a mild stomach disorder. Shortly afterward, the child died of an aspirin overdose, and the parents sued the doctor.

During the trial, it came out that the father had found an empty aspirin bottle near his stricken child. He hadn't informed the doctor of this, however, and the court ruled that the physician could hardly be held liable for something he didn't know. Moreover, the doctor's records showed that he had closely questioned the father about anything that might have caused the child's disorder, and the distraught parent hadn't mentioned the aspirin bottle.

• In a very similar case, a father took his 15-month-old daughter to the family physician. The father had reason to think the child had eaten a quantity of aspirin, but he simply told the doctor she was "sick." The doctor knew that the girl's mother was suffering from flu, so he figured the child had contracted the same disease.

Later, the child died from aspirin overdose, and the parents sued the doctor. On the surface, it appeared the doctor had a pretty good case. After all, the father *had* failed to provide pertinent information.

It didn't turn out to be that simple. An expert medical witness for the parents testified that the child had been hyperventilating to an extreme extent when the doctor examined her. This, the witness stated, should have warned the doctor that some problem other than flu existed, and the proper course would have been to examine the patient further. Consequently, the doctor was held liable.

Moral: If the information a doctor gets for a diagnosis seems inaccurate or incomplete, or if it doesn't square with his own observations, he's responsible for making reasonable further examination.

One other suggestion: Since a large number of errors in diagnosis stem from the fact that the patient has been drinking, don't be too quick to blame all the symptoms on alcohol. That can backfire. A typical example:

A taxi driver was brought to a doctor after a car crash. Smelling booze on the patient's breath, the doctor shook his head in disgust—which was noted by the patient's brother—and did a quick, inadequate examination.

The brother was then advised to take the patient home and return the next day "after he's sobered up." The patient didn't last until the next day. He died within a few hours of undetected subdural hematoma, and the doctor was subsequently sued for malpractice.

Call in a consultant if necessary

Ego plays a big role here. A physician is handling a difficult case—perhaps one that's even out of his field—and he says to himself, "I don't need any help. I can manage this myself."

Well, maybe he can and maybe he can't. The point is, if he can't, he'll probably have a high price to pay. Take the following case:

An attorney was playing with his children in the family swimming pool. After sliding down a chute, he complained of a violent headache. His family physician diagnosed the problem as a slight neck sprain. The attorney's wife, an RN, asked the doctor to call in a neurological consultant, but he declined, saying, "I've seen enough of these things to know what I'm talking about."

A few days later, the attorney was driving to work when he passed out. He was taken to a hospital emergency room, where a CT scan was taken. Reading the scan, a neurosurgeon concluded that the attorney had an aneurysm of the brain that had burst. The attorney died shortly afterward.

The family physician has now been sued by the family for failing to make a proper diagnosis. The plaintiff's lawyer says, "Our medical experts tell us that a neurosurgeon or a neurologist would have immediately suspected an aneurysm, conducted an angiography, and operated, with a 98 percent chance of the patient surviving without disability."

Since the deceased attorney was earning well over $100,000 a year and was only 42 years old when he died, a settlement or jury award in the $5-million range would not be surprising. That's the sort of high price I mentioned previously.

If a doctor in a situation such as this goes to trial, what can he expect? An item in the *Journal of the American Medical Association* answers that question right on the nail:

"When a physician defends a professional liability suit on the basis of his honest mistake in diagnosis or judgment as to the course of treatment, he is essentially arguing that in his management of the patient he did what other physicians in the community would have done under the same circumstances. He should be prepared to meet allegations that he was not knowledgeable, was indecisive, and failed to initiate required diagnostic tests and therapy. His experience and training will be sharply questioned, and he can expect to be called upon for an explanation as to why he did not relinquish responsibility for the patient to another physician. In cases in which consultation was sought, the physician, of course, would be in a better position to show that the diagnosis was not superficial and that alternative possibilities were carefully eliminated in the treatment of the patient."

That pretty well wraps up diagnosis. What about medication errors? We'll go into that next.

13

The medication minefield

A drug that's wrongly prescribed can have painful side effects for you—a session on the witness stand to explain what went wrong.

I once listened to a noted professor of medicine lecture on what he termed the "perils of prescribing." Too many doctors, he said, have too little respect for "that innocent-looking little blob we call a pill. It can work wonders, but if it's not controlled, it can also wreck lives—just as a truck out of control can wreck lives. It's a doctor's duty to know that pill, to understand it, to respect it—and most important of all, to control it by prescribing with extreme care."

That's good practical advice, legally as well as medically, and many courts have concurred with it. As the Supreme Court of the state of Washington once put it, a physician is a "learned intermediary" between the manufacturer of a drug and the patient for whom it's prescribed. If the patient is harmed by the drug, then the doctor will have to answer as to how "learned" he really is.

By that, I don't just mean the doctor's knowledge of the drug. The manner in which he prescribed it will also be considered. For example:

A physician wrote seven separate prescriptions for Tuinal over a two-month period for a 17-year-old girl. When the girl went to a drugstore to fill the last prescription, her dazed condition worried the pharmacist. He called the doctor, who snapped, "Fill the damn thing and stop bothering me. I'm busy."

A day later, the girl died of an overdose of the drug.

The doctor was then hit from three sides—a malpractice suit, a criminal charge, and action by state authorities to revoke his license. He lost on all counts, and ended up in prison for involuntary manslaughter.

Few doctors are that cavalier or brutal, but many are sued for indiscriminate prescribing. A careless attitude toward refills and renewals is a principal cause of these suits.

In a typical case, a man was on a medication for hypertension for 14 years. Never once in that time did his attending physician test him for possible ill effects from the drug. The patient finally died of a liver disease that was aggravated by the medication.

The doctor, sued by the family, could only defend himself by saying the patient had never complained of any ill effects, so he had simply continued to renew and refill the prescription. That was a totally inadequate defense, and the suit was settled out of court for what was believed to be in the million-dollar range.

In another case, a woman came to a GP with complaints of anxiety and insomnia. He put her on tranquilizers and sleeping pills. For more than a year, the doctor renewed or refilled prescriptions simply on the woman's requests. She finally died of a drug overdose.

The family then sued the GP for malpractice. During the trial, two pertinent facts came out: (1) Other physicians were prescribing for the woman, something the GP hadn't bothered to ask about. (2) A psychiatrist in the same building as the GP had been treating the woman for depression. The GP had known about this, but he'd never checked with the psychiatrist about the patient's drug-taking history and emotional condition.

Along with losing the malpractice suit, the GP had his medical license suspended for six months and was placed on probation for five years.

A few suggestions: Carefully monitor patients during drug therapy, especially if it's for a chronic or long-term-care condition. Be prudent when renewing or refilling prescriptions. Ask all new patients what medications they're taking and whether other doctors are prescribing for them.

If another doctor is covering for you, notify him that he should limit prescription refills for your patients to immediate needs. Follow the same policy if you're covering for another physician.

Here are other danger areas in the medication minefield:

Side effects and allergic reactions

I'm a close observer of jurors, and I can read a lot from their facial expressions and body language. I remember one case in which those expressions came through loud and clear.

The defendant doctor was accused of negligence in prescribing a potent drug to a patient who subsequently died of a side effect. On the stand, the doctor said he "just didn't know" about that particular side effect.

I glanced at the jurors. About half had raised their eyes to the high heavens. The other half were squirming in irritation.

I knew right then the doctor was going to lose, and I knew exactly why. Jurors look with extreme disfavor on doctors who prescribe drugs without knowing of possible side effects—or, if they don't know, not looking them up. An example:

A young model came to an internist with a complaint of periodic acne. He prescribed a combination of a medicated cleanser and a skin preparation. In a short while, the preparation caused redness and a burning sensation on the patient's face. When she reported this to the internist, he advised her to reduce the amount of medication but to continue its use.

Eventually the irritation became so bad that it left scars on the patient's nose and cheeks. She then sued the doctor, claiming that her career as a model was threatened.

In his defense, the doctor insisted he hadn't known that scarring was a possible side effect of the medication. The plaintiff's lawyer promptly produced a package insert that warned medication should be discontinued if the patient showed any hypersensitivity to it—"otherwise, scarring may occur."

The doctor's only response was that he "couldn't recall" reading the warning—and that, anyway, the patient should have read it herself. His insurance carrier, fully realizing the adverse emotional effect all this would have on the jury, headed off what would probably have been a whopping award by settling the matter.

A doctor in another case didn't escape that easily—he was walloped with the heaviest part of a $9-million jury verdict. The trouble began when a young woman was undergoing a rhinoplasty. The surgeon insisted that the anesthesia should include a drug that could affect a patient's cough reflex—a danger so well-known that few surgeons in that locality used the drug.

Because of this, the nurse-anesthetist objected to the use of the drug, but the doctor told her to shut up. During the operation, the patient lost her cough reflex, complications soon followed, and the woman suffered brain damage that left her a spastic quadriplegic.

Less dramatic events can also lead to disastrous results, particularly if the doctor knows of side effects but doesn't tell the patient about them. An illustration:

A young housewife crashed her car after she fell asleep while driving to a supermarket with her three children. Mother and children were all injured. The cause of the crash, she contended in a malpractice complaint, was a tranquilizer that an internist had prescribed for her.

In deposition, the doctor was asked, "Did you warn the patient that the tranquilizer could cause drowsiness and that she shouldn't drive a car while using it?"

"No," the doctor replied. "I thought everybody knew that. Besides, I was sure the pharmacist would put the usual warning label on the bottle."

The pharmacist hadn't put the label on the bottle, but that didn't reduce the doctor's responsibility. The case was settled for half a million dollars.

Suggestions: In the eyes of the law, there's simply no excuse for ignorance about possible medication side effects, since the *Physicians' Desk Reference* and other sources of information are readily available. The doctor also has recourse to such educational materials as the AMA's Patient Medication Information program.

Your drug-related liability risks will be minimized if you supplement these sources with your own plain-English warning to the patient on possible side effects. Then make sure the patient understands what you're talking about.

Also make certain—*before* you start drug therapy—that the patient understands when you ask about drug allergies. This confuses some patients, who figure that you mean something like hay fever. Make clear you're inquiring about an allergic reaction or sensitivity to the medication that you intend to prescribe.

Administration of the drug

Very often a problem arises from a misunderstanding by a medical assistant. For example, a physician ordered an antibiotic given I.V. The nurse administered it I.M., causing a severe reaction at the site of the injection. Result: The doctor and the nurse were named in a malpractice suit.

In another case, a doctor prescribed Lanoxin for a hospitalized child, who died after an injection by a nurse. A written order, produced by the doctor in evidence, read, "Give 3.0cc Lanoxin today for one dose only." That was fine, but it didn't go far enough—it should have specified that the medication be administered orally in liquid form.

The nurse, who was familiar with the drug only in smaller doses, gave it by injection. In that mode of administration, the larger dose was fatal. The doctor and nurse were both held liable.

Suggestions: First, check the proper administration of a drug—it's contained in the manufacturer's brochure, also on the package or bottle. If an assistant is administering the drug, make sure she knows the right mode. In addition, assistants should be familiar with the purpose and common dosages of medications.

Dosage

Most doctors are knowledgeable enough to start a patient off on drug therapy at a lower level of dosage, then work up to a higher one if necessary for maximum efficiency. Occasionally, however, a physician will shoot for the top level right off. If the drug is potent, that can be harmful, and the doctor will have difficulty in defending the treatment.

Another problem crops up when a doctor neglects to regularly query a patient—especially one in long-term therapy—about how the medication is working. Here are three ways that doctors have lost malpractice cases because of that failure: (1) The drug turned out to be ineffective. (2) The dosage was wrong. (3) The diagnosis was erroneous in the first place.

A further suggestion: When giving patients drug samples, as many doctors do out of the goodness of their hearts, check the dosage on the package. Samples of different dosages sometimes come in look-alike packages.

Handwriting

The doctor scrawl is a basis of jokes, but nobody laughs when a patient is harmed because of an illegible prescription. In one case, an internist scribbled a hospital order for a pain medication to be taken once a day (q.d.). The order was interpreted as q.i.d.—four times a day—and the patient was overdosed. The case was settled for $75,000.

Suggestions: If your handwriting is hard to read, print prescriptions and medication orders. It may take a little more time, but it could save you a lot of trouble.

- Be especially careful when prescribing similarly spelled drugs, such as digoxin and digitoxin.

And don't get huffy when a nurse or pharmacist checks back with you to verify an unclear prescription or order—*encourage* them to backstop you.

Documentation

In a malpractice complaint against a doctor, a patient claimed she'd told him she was allergic to penicillin. He said she'd informed him to the contrary, but he'd "forgotten" to note that in the medical record. He lost the case, as have many other doctors who failed to keep good medication records.

Suggestions: When a drug is prescribed, write it on the chart, along with dosage, method of administration, and any refills. If there's any change in dosage, document it, as well as the patient's progress, or lack of progress, on that therapy.

It's a good idea to use prescription blanks with duplicates that can be placed in the patient's file. Also consider a basic medication sheet that can be attached to the file jacket, forming a handy reference to drugs prescribed, dosages, and dates.

More about the importance of good medical records—much more—in the next chapter.

14

*D*on't drop time bombs in your medical files

Good records are the keystone of a solid malpractice defense. Bad records can blow that foundation apart.

Here's one example of how important your medical records are in the eyes of the law: The New York Court of Appeals upheld a six-month suspension of a doctor's medical license for failure to maintain charts that accurately reflected his evaluation and treatment of patients.

Records, the court held, aren't just skimpy notes scribbled by the treating physician for his own use—they're expected to be clear and detailed enough to provide meaningful information to other practitioners who might treat the patient.

Those same records, it's important to note, might also be scanned by lawyers seeking fuel for litigation.

Most physicians know what good records should contain— relevant dates, nature of the complaint, results of examinations and tests, diagnosis (if it's uncertain, designate it as "provisional"), and prognosis, if one can be made. However, even if a physician fulfills those basic requirements, he can still go astray. Here's how:

Indiscreet remarks

The doctor on the stand was doing well until his medical records were introduced into the malpractice trial. One note identified the plaintiff as a "fatso" who "should take off at least 30 pounds—but she'd rather eat her head off."

Although the issue of obesity had nothing to do with the charge against the doctor, he lost the case. Jurors undoubtedly felt that he was unobjective and unkind in his attitude toward the patient. And, I might add, he was certainly unthinking in writing his feelings into the patient's file.

The fact is, when a doctor uses medical records to refresh his memory while testifying, those records become part of the evidence. The opposition lawyer can examine and comment on them—even read portions to the jury.

You can imagine the reaction of jurors when they hear such comments as, "This guy's heart is OK but his head sure needs examining." "The patient is a very active female—with a mouth to match." "Another crock. Get rid of him as soon as possible." Those are all excerpts from actual cases.

Privileged material

A doctor accused of malpractice was discussing the case with his lawyer.

"What we need at this point is your own critical evaluation of all that transpired," the lawyer said. "Go back over the case and write down anything that might be construed as unfavorable to you. Let's look at the worst things that might be said against you. Then we can decide how to deal with them."

This is not unusual—lawyers quite often ask clients to act as devil's advocates. In this instance, though, the legal strategy backfired. After writing down his thoughts on possible weak-

nesses in his defense, the doctor sent the report off to his lawyer and dropped a copy in the plaintiff's medical file.

Later, when the plaintiff's attorney subpoenaed the file, he
hit a veritable jackpot—a detailed account in the doctor's own
words of how he might have gone wrong in his treatment of
the patient. The doctor lost the case.

Keep in mind that letters, reports, and notes of conversations between a doctor and his lawyer are confidential. They
should be placed in a privileged file, which is not subject to
subpoena.

Actually, you should be careful about placing anything in a
medical file that's not directly related to the care and treatment of the patient. One physician deposited in a female patient's file some affectionate letters from her that were later
used by the doctor's wife as ammunition in a divorce battle.

Changing the record

If you spot an error on a patient's medical chart, you have a
right to correct it. That's simply a matter of setting the record
straight. Within limits, you also have a right to edit the record
to clarify some aspect of your treatment.

However, if it appears that your intention is to edit *out* evidence against you, you might be in trouble. No matter how
minor the changes may be, they could weight the balance of a
case against you.

And if you deliberately alter a chart to make yourself look
better—well, that's surefire trouble. In one case, a doctor re-
constructed the dates of procedures performed on a patient.
His creativity collapsed, though, when he put down a treatment date of February 29 in what was not a leap year.

In another case, a doctor won a jury verdict partly because
his records looked so authentic. Later, after filing a post-trial
motion to set aside the verdict, the plaintiff's attorney established that the record forms hadn't been printed at the time
the doctor treated the patient. The favorable verdict was cancelled, and the doctor's insurer settled out of court.

If you have good reason to correct the record, don't obliterate the original notes. Just stroke lightly through them, so they can still be read. Then write in your additional material, along with the date of the correction, and initial it.

Messy records

An obstetrician accused of malpractice was asked to produce his post-op notes for the case. He couldn't because he'd scribbled them on his surgical gown and absentmindedly tossed it in the laundry.

Few doctors are *that* careless in their record-keeping, but many are still at fault. Witness the following cases:

• An internist testified emphatically that he remembered clearly what had transpired during an examination of the patient who was suing him for malpractice.

"Do you have documentation for that?" the plaintiff's attorney asked.

"I certainly do." The internist handed over the chart to the attorney, who scanned it, frowned, shook his head, and finally gave up.

"I can't make heads or tails of this," the attorney said, handing the record back to the internist. "You read it."

The internist started out quite strongly, then faltered, backtracked, tried again, became lost, and weakly admitted he couldn't read his own records.

• A surgeon carried his medical records to the stand in a neat-looking file folder. When he opened it, however, he produced several postcards and a lot of scribbled figures on scraps of paper before getting to the pertinent record.

"What are those?" the plaintiff's attorney asked, pointing to the postcards.

"The plaintiff sent them to me when he was on vacations," the doctor replied. "They show we used to be friends."

"And those?" the attorney went on, pointing at the scribbled figures.

"Oh, those." The doctor looked at them and scratched his head. "Well, I sometimes balance my checkbook between patients, and I guess these just got in the wrong place."

The jury figured that he was in the wrong himself, and found against him.

Moral: When jurors see a doctor is messy with his record-keeping, they'll probably figure he's messy in other aspects of his practice as well. So write your records legibly on charts of uniform size. Arrange them in sequence for ready reference, and place them in neat folders. And keep irrelevant or "junk" material out of the files.

Trying to be a good guy

This is an admirable trait, but not when it comes to recording medical findings. A GP found that out the hard way when, at a patient's request, he didn't record a history of alcoholism.

Later, when the patient required an operation, the surgeon checked the medical records and found no contraindication to surgery. However, the patient received an anesthetic that adversely reacted to the patient's alcoholic liver, and he died on the operating table. The GP, the anesthesiologist, and the surgeon were all sued.

When the GP was asked why he failed to record the patient's alcoholism, he testified, "I was trying to save him from embarrassment if ever his chart should be seen by a third party, such as an insurance company."

That wasn't good enough for the jury, which returned a million-dollar award against the three doctors.

Trying to cover up a colleague's blunder can also be costly. Take the radiologist who saw on an X-ray that a surgical clamp had been left in a patient after an operation.

"There's a clamp in there," he told the surgeon by telephone. "Better get it out."

The clamp was not removed, and the patient died. When the facts about the clamp were discovered by the family, they sued the surgeon, the radiologist, and the hospital. In a deposition, the radiologist stated, "I didn't record the presence of the clamp because I didn't want to get anybody in trouble."

You can imagine how a jury would have viewed that sort of defense. The case was settled out of court for a large sum.

Moral: Good guys of this type finish last in court. Covering up for a colleague or a patient is dangerous. The physician who attempts to hide pertinent facts frequently winds up in trouble himself.

Overlooking lab results

This happens quite often. A physician is busy or distracted, and fails to note significant test results. Then when he's sued and goes back in the record to find out what happened, there's nothing there.

An internist who was caught in that sort of bind told the jury, "I distinctly remember ordering blood gases for the patient. The results arrived late, and I didn't get around to them in time to find that the blood gases had dropped. I'm extremely sorry the patient died, but I was very busy at the time."

He had no documentation to back up his testimony, and the plaintiff's lawyer brought out damaging evidence: The "late" results of the test had been available in the hospital long before the "busy" internist had hurried off for an "important engagement"—a medical society dinner.

Anticipating the jury's negative response to that revelation, and the general lack of documentation, the defense attorney recommended a settlement.

In the next chapter, we'll go into another kind of record—informed consent.

15

*H*ow informed consent can backfire on you

The patients consent may seem valid, but it can explode when put to a legal test.

In more than 50 years as a trial lawyer, I've been involved in hundreds of cases in which doctors thought they'd obtained ironclad informed consent. When the courtroom jousting had ended, however, many of these doctors found their ironclad shields were made of tissue paper.

One instance: A surgeon sat down with a woman who needed a total abdominal hysterectomy. He fully explained the procedure to her, including possible risks.

"Do you understand all that?" the doctor asked.

"I think so," she replied.

"Then you'll sign the consent form?"

"Yes."

The doctor then left the examining room, and the nurse came in with the form. The patient looked just a little dubious, so the nurse asked, "Is everything all right?"

"Oh, I guess so," the woman replied, "but this must be a very dangerous operation. Otherwise, you wouldn't be asking me to sign this form."

The nurse responded, "Oh, don't worry about that—it's just routine. Nothing will go wrong."

The woman signed. During the operation, something did go wrong. The surgeon nicked the bladder, resulting in a vesicovaginal fistula. Now, nicking the bladder in a complicated hysterectomy is not necessarily negligent. Moreover, in this case, the doctor had a seemingly strong defense—the patient's signed consent form, which listed the possibility of a vesicovaginal fistula.

The plaintiff's attorney destroyed that defense by highlighting the nurse's statement: "Nothing will go wrong." That, the attorney contended, invalidated the consent.

The doctor argued that the nurse was young and inexperienced about legal implications. That, the plaintiff's attorney countered, was all the more reason why the doctor should have made a special effort to teach her about such matters. The doctor lost the case.

Two morals: First, it's not enough for a doctor himself to keep up to date on the often tricky issue of informed consent. Key members of the doctor's staff, who act as his agents, should also be educated.

Second, informed consent is a contract. If a doctor induces someone to enter into it by promising a reward or immunity from risk, he loads that contract against himself.

There are many other ways, of course, that a physician can get into trouble over informed consent. Let's look at them, and then at some ways to protect yourself against them.

When the patient is rushed

In a typical instance, an OBG knew well in advance that a patient was going to require a Caesarean section. Yet the doctor waited until the night before the operation to get informed consent. What's more, he took a jocular approach.

"Here's a little something from the legal department," he said. "Sign it and let's get it over with. You don't want to hold up the parade in the morning, do you?"

The patient had just been admitted to the hospital and was still somewhat bewildered. The doctor's attitude, which indicated the consent process was a mere formality, confused her further.

Also, as she started to read the consent form, an administrative nurse came to the bedside and remarked impatiently, "Isn't that finished yet? I should be off duty right now."

The pressure may have been unintentional, but it made the woman sign the form without reading it all.

During the operation, the obstetrician lacerated the intestinal tract, and the woman later sued. In court, the doctor pointed out that she had signed the consent form and must have known that the laceration was a risk.

As the woman's attorney, I replied that although she had signed the consent form, she had hardly been properly informed. Nor had she been given adequate time to weigh the risks. A jury found in her favor.

In another instance, a middle-aged bachelor asked to consult with members of his family in another city before consenting to an operation.

"Well, we can," the doctor told him, "but I have my own schedule to keep to, you know, and we can't dawdle forever. I've told you the operation is for your own good. Isn't that enough?"

The patient then signed a consent form.

Later, he sued the doctor because of complications from the surgery. He won, largely because the jury felt he'd been pressured into the operation and should have been *encouraged*— not merely allowed—to consult with his relatives.

Jurors, incidentally, often identify with patients who've been adversely influenced by the hurry-up atmosphere of many medical offices and hospitals. They've been in the same situation themselves.

When the patient is distraught

"If you don't have this operation," the doctor warned the patient, "you'll die." Thus, the woman was literally scared into having a mastectomy. As she signed the consent form, she was sobbing so bitterly that a nurse had to guide her hand.

After the operation, the woman suffered severe depression along with physical ailments.

On her behalf, I sued the doctor, who tried to defend himself with the signed consent form. It didn't work. I argued successfully that he had obtained the consent by frightening the patient. I also pointed out that the woman had not really been in control of herself when she signed.

She won a large settlement.

When the patient is sedated

This happens with surprising frequency. I know of one case in which a patient was actually awakened from sedation to sign a consent form.

In another case, a stapedectomy patient was being wheeled into the operating room when a form was thrust at him. It listed three principal risks—partial or complete loss of hearing, dizziness or loss of balance, and constant ringing in the ears. The patient was so highly sedated, however, that his signature was just a wiggly line.

After the operation, the patient lost all hearing, and the consent form became an issue in a subsequent lawsuit. I represented him and had no difficulty in having the "informed consent" ruled invalid.

No judge or jury will hold anyone to a contract that is signed in a semiconscious state.

When there's a language barrier

Most doctors know they need to be careful when dealing with foreign-born patients, who often need help in communicating. But trouble can also crop up when a doctor encounters an American-born patient with a limited knowledge and understanding of the English language. For example: A woman was scheduled for a sterilization procedure. Ten minutes before the operation, she signed a consent form. Her husband had previously signed the same form, which stated that sterilization procedures sometimes cause complications.

That's what happened in this case, and the couple sued several doctors and the hospital. The defense presented evidence that the man and wife had both read the consent form and signed it.

Witnesses for the plaintiffs, however, testified that both were practically illiterate. Neither of them had been educated beyond the third grade in an Appalachian backwoods school. They "read" only the simplest of words, and a scrawled signature was about all they could "write."

Under those circumstances, the court decided, the form did not constitute valid informed consent, and the couple won the case.

When alternative treatment is available

The symptoms were classic—difficulty in breathing, a suffocating feeling, excruciating chest pain.

"Angina," the GP told the middle-aged stockbroker. "You'll need a coronary bypass."

The patient was then referred to a surgeon, who confirmed the GP's diagnosis and arranged for the operation. Both doctors were on hand when the patient signed a consent form. He later stated, "They gave me the impression that surgery was the only hope I had."

The four-hour operation was not a success, and the cost was steep—about $20,000. Still in pain, the stockbroker went to a cardiologist, who put him on a drug regimen. This controlled the condition to some extent, and greatly relieved the pain.

The stockbroker then sued the GP and the surgeon. In their defense, the doctors produced the consent form, which clearly stated that coronary bypasses did not always have successful outcomes.

Maybe so, countered the plaintiff, but if he'd known that drugs were available to control this condition, he wouldn't have had the operation. He won.

When a doctor goes beyond the scope of the consent

There's a fine line here, and I'll define it by showing two different cases.

In the first, the patient signed a consent form for an appendectomy. During the operation, the surgeon discovered some enlarged follicular cysts on the ovaries. Knowing that the cysts could grow to a dangerous size, he punctured them.

Later, the patient sued the surgeon, claiming the puncturing of the cysts had been unauthorized. Technically, the patient was right—the consent form had mentioned only the appendectomy.

However, the court ruled in the doctor's favor, commenting, "What was the surgeon to do when he found abnormal cysts...that were potentially dangerous? Was it his duty to leave her unconscious on the operating table, doff his operating habiliments, and go forth to find someone with authority to consent to the extended operation? The potential danger was evident to a skilled surgeon....Reason and common sense dictated that he should do just what he did."

Contrast this with the second case, in which a surgeon removed a patient's fallopian tubes during an appendectomy. The patient sued on grounds that she had not given consent to the removal of the tubes.

This court sided with the patient, ruling that there had been no immediate emergency that would justify removal of the tubes without the consent of the patient or her stepmother: "Although delay might have proved harmful, there was still time to give the parent and the patient the opportunity to weigh the fateful question."

Many courts agree that if a doctor, during an authorized procedure, discovers an emergency or unanticipated condition requiring immediate action to preserve the patient's life or health, he has good legal ground to correct the condition.

Other courts have held that extending a procedure is justified as long as the patient gives a general consent, authorizing the doctor to exercise his judgment to remedy any unforeseen circumstance or injurious condition.

How to protect yourself

All of the situations I've described show how doctors or their agents can create damaging loopholes in informed consent. Avoiding the circumstances that set up those situations is the best way to make sure the loopholes are closed. Here are nine points to keep in mind:

1. The law clearly states that a patient has the absolute right to decide whether a medical procedure shall be performed on him. That right is automatically invaded by a doctor who obtains consent through intimidation, coercion, misrepresentation, or inducement. Consent is also rendered invalid if the patient is not in full possession of his faculties.

2. In obtaining consent, a doctor should discard paternalistic, authoritarian roles and act as a teacher, advocate, and counselor. Give the patient ample time to weigh the risks, encourage him to ask questions, and involve the family whenever possible.

Pick a quiet setting for this discussion, where the patient isn't likely to become anxious or distracted. And never leave the discussion to the last minute.

3. Use simple English, avoiding technical terms or medical jargon. Always ask if the patient understands what you've told him. No contract is valid if it's not understood by those entering into it. Record the gist of the discussion.

4. If you or your hospital uses preprinted consent forms, make sure they're understandable. One study shows that 61 percent of such forms required a college-level education to comprehend certain passages. Only 31 percent of the national population has had any college education.

5. Give the patient all the information he needs to know about the procedure, then allow him to decide whether it should be carried out.

Guidelines? At a minimum, you must disclose risks of death and serious bodily harm.

In some instances, you may be justified in not disclosing all material risks—when an emergency exists, or when the patient might become so upset that his treatment would be hindered, or he'd be incapable of making a rational choice.

Slight risks need not always be mentioned. One court said, "In some involved procedures it's obviously prohibitive and unrealistic to expect physicians to discuss with patients every risk of proposed treatment no matter how small or remote."

6. Though written consent is preferable, oral consent is just as legally valid. Oral consent, however, is usually harder to prove—and easier for the patient to deny later. Try to have at least one witness present, and document in writing what the patient says.

Some doctors tape record informed consent. That's a good idea *provided* the patient knows what's happening. Make sure the recorder is in plain sight, explain to the patient why it's there, then turn it on only after the patient has agreed to the recording. Repeat that agreement as soon as the recorder is running.

7. A patient may waive his right to be informed about the risks of a procedure. If so, be doubly sure you document it.

8. Remember that when jurors are presented with sloppily obtained informed consent, they're likely to think, "Well, if the doctor was negligent in this respect, he might be negligent in others." Once that seed of doubt is planted, the plaintiff's attorneys will make sure it grows.

9. In obtaining informed consent, ask yourself three questions: Was the patient really informed? Did he consent willingly and voluntarily? Was it truly a free act?

If the answers are all Yes, the consent has a good chance of holding up in court.

Your defense also has a better chance of holding up if you deal correctly with second opinions, the subject of the next chapter.

16

Second opinions: a growing malpractice threat

It's often helpful to obtain another doctor's opinion, but it can be harmful to reject it.

Many malpractice cases stem from a doctor's failure to call for—and heed— outside help. It's sometimes a matter of professional pride. A doctor figures, "What the hell—what can a consultant tell me that I don't already know?" Too often, that attitude results in a jury telling the doctor something he didn't know—that it's wise to get a second opinion.

Furthermore, more and more health insurance carriers are insisting on second opinions as a means of holding down costs. At the same time, second opinions are opening up a whole new area of liability for doctors.

The problem usually starts when a doctor brushes aside a second opinion. "The insurance company asked for this guy's opinion—I didn't," the doctor grumbles. "So I don't have to do it his way—I'll do it mine."

What happens if the doctor's procedure then causes harm to the patient? A jury answered that question clearly in a recent California case that's been described as "a breakthrough for plaintiffs."

The patient, a 50-year-old mechanic, was referred to an orthopedic surgeon after he injured his left knee at work. The surgeon aspirated 40cc of fluid from the knee and prescribed physical therapy.

Several months later, when the patient was still complaining of intense pain, the surgeon discovered a torn meniscus and did a meniscectomy. That didn't help, either—nor did cortisone injections, anti-inflammatory medications, and splinting.

The surgeon then decided that a total knee resection was necessary, with placement of a prosthesis. The patient's insurance carrier wasn't so sure about that—it wanted a second opinion from a prominent orthopedist. He examined the patient and sent a written report to the surgeon, recommending arthroscopy.

The surgeon later claimed he showed the consultant's report to the patient and discussed it with him, stating, "I explained that arthroscopy was primarily a diagnostic procedure, and said we'd already seen the inside of the knee joint several months earlier. After discussing all the options, the patient felt that total replacement was the most logical choice."

This conversation, however, was not documented in the patient's chart.

After the total replacement was performed, the knee was still painful, with diminished range of motion. The patient eventually went to another physician, who removed the prosthesis and fused the knee.

That relieved the pain, but it left the patient with a limp. He had to use a cane to get about; he was unable to return to work, and he couldn't engage in sports that he'd previously enjoyed. He was hard-up financially, too—his workers' compensation was far less than he'd earned from his job, and he had five children to support.

In addition, the patient's mental attitude deteriorated. A psychiatrist diagnosed him as suffering from depression and traumatic neurosis, with strong feelings of hostility toward the surgeon, whom he blamed for his predicament.

The patient then consulted Beverly Hills attorney David R. Glickman about the possibility of suing the surgeon.

"At that time, jury verdicts for unnecessary procedures were uncommon," Glickman recalls. "I had to find some special circumstance that would give the plaintiff a fair chance of winning."

He discovered it in the surgeon's file on the patient—in the second-opinion report from the consultant.

"That gave me the special circumstance I was looking for," says Glickman. "The treating doctor had proceeded with a major operation against the advice of a highly qualified consultant. I figured a jury would want to know why."

In the resulting suit, the surgeon was accused of negligently diagnosing and treating the patient's knee injury, ignoring the second opinion that advised against total replacement surgery, and not informing the patient fully about the risks of the operation.

The surgeon denied all the charges. At trial, he produced two expert witnesses who testified there had been no deviation from normal standard of care. On the stand, the surgeon himself stated that the operation constituted reasonable treatment. He had proceeded with the surgery, he said, because he was qualified to make that medical judgment.

This, however, was contested by attorney Glickman, who produced evidence to show that the surgeon (1) had been out of residency only $2^{1}/_{2}$ years when he performed the operation, and (2) this was the first total knee resection he had done in private practice.

At that point, the second opinion in the case became crucial. The consultant who had made it was now dead, but his written report was introduced as evidence.

"Did you have this second opinion in your files?" Glickman asked the surgeon.

"Yes," he replied.

That testimony helped to sway the jury, which returned a $667,550 award for the plaintiff. This was reduced by $175,000 because of workers' compensation that had already been received by the patient.

The surgeon made a motion for a new trial, but it was denied. However, he did obtain from the court an order stating that "the judgment...does not relate to a breach of integrity or any lack of professional competence or training on the part of the defendant."

After the trial, there was an interesting cross fire between the attorney and the surgeon.

Glickman: "This case is a breakthrough for plaintiffs. It opens up a whole new area in medical malpractice."

The surgeon: "The only breakthrough is the ability to obtain an award from a jury not for malpractice or negligence, but because of a poor result of surgery."

Another view is expressed by David S. Rubsamen, a California lawyer and physician who edits the Professional Liability Newsletter: "Without the second-opinion doctor's report in evidence, this case might well have gone the other way. The lesson is clear: Where a consultation does not support an important therapeutic intervention, the referring physician will be well advised to obtain further consultation before deciding to proceed."

Physicians will also be well advised to use extreme care in referring a patient to a hospital emergency room. More on that in the following chapter.

17

Your liability when you direct a patient to the ER

If you think you can pass your responsibilities along with the patient, think again.

Not too many years ago, a doctor couldn't get onto a hospital medical staff unless he agreed to serve time in the emergency room. That was a considerable burden—not only because of the often messy chores that had to be performed, but because of liability risks. Imagine the foreboding of, say, a psychiatrist or dermatologist who had to come in and look after everything from a bloody nose to broken toes.

Today, thanks to the specialists in emergency medicine who staff many ERs, that sort of liability has largely disappeared. However, it's been replaced by a danger that's even trickier because some doctors don't even realize it's there. They figure, "Well, I'll just refer this patient to the ER and let them deal with it," assuming that any liability involved will rest solely with the hospital.

That isn't necessarily so. Statistics show that about one in every five malpractice claims closed against hospitals involves the emergency room—which means that if you send a patient to the ER and a complaint results, you just might be a malpractice statistic yourself.

Reveals David Karp, a California authority on this sort of liability: "As a malpractice-prevention adviser, I'm often asked to survey emergency rooms for potential malpractice problems. During those surveys, I've discovered many cases of how carelessly some physicians use the ER."

"Carelessly" is putting it mildly. I know of one case in which a patient called his doctor's office for an appointment and was instructed instead to go to a nearby ER "because the doctor is busy." Actually, it developed later, the doctor wasn't all that busy—he just didn't want to see the patient because of some personal differences they'd had.

At the ER, after a considerable wait, the patient's complaint was diagnosed as a "slight" cardiac condition. It wasn't all that slight. The patient died the next day, and the family sued the hospital and the referring doctor. The case was settled out of court for $500,000, half of which was assessed against the "busy" doctor, who was accused of abandonment.

Most doctors, of course, are much more considerate and caring than that, but some still get in trouble in directing patients to the ER. Here are the principal ways that can happen.

When the patient is wrongly admitted to the hospital

This usually occurs when the doctor regards the ER as a satellite office where he can pass along cases that are inconvenient for him to handle. However, if it's necessary to admit the patient to the hospital, the admission orders usually have to be written by the attending physician—that is, the patient's regular doctor. Too often, the attending gets the ER doctor to write the order—and that can backfire. One example:

• The referred patient arrived at the ER in an agitated state. The doctor on duty was unable to diagnose the problem but felt the patient should be hospitalized. The patient's regular physician agreed to that by phone, then persuaded the ER doctor to write the admission orders because "I just don't have time right now."

Later that night in the hospital, the patient suffered a stroke, which left him partially disabled. In the malpractice suit that followed, it was revealed that the ER physician, with a very limited knowledge of the patient's medical history, had written sketchy admission orders that had hampered proper follow-up care.

The finger of blame also pointed to the attending physician, who did not conform to hospital policy in writing admission orders himself. In failing to do so, he lost a valuable defense to the charges against him. The case was settled out of court.

When documentation is deficient

Very often, a doctor refers a patient to the ER because facilities there are more suitable for certain procedures. The doctor then comes along, attends to the patient, and returns to his normal routine. Sometimes, though, he leaves behind a legal time bomb—little or no record of what he'd done in the ER.

Here's an illustrative case. A doctor came to the ER to attend to one of his patients, a victim of a car crash. A number of lacerations were repaired, and the patient was sent home.

Subsequently, the patient suffered vascular compromise, which led to amputation of the left leg. The attending doctor, when sued for malpractice, contended the occlusion had occurred after the patient left the ER.

The doctor, however, had no documentation to support his claim. He could only say, "I didn't take notes because I thought somebody else at the ER would do that."

Nobody did—that was the doctor's own responsibility—and he had to settle the suit for $500,000.

The point to remember is that the documentation for cases handled in the ER should be as complete as cases handled in your own office.

When communication is lacking

The ER is a high-pressure place, and doctors in private practice can often be busy, too. Add to this the fact that the telephone doesn't always provide a clear line of communication, and you come up with a potential problem. For example:

• A family physician was called away from a patient in his office to answer a pressing query from an ER doctor, who said, "I understand you're Mr. So-and-So's physician."

"That's right."

"Well, he's been brought in here with a stomach complaint. He's in quite a bit of pain, so I haven't been able to get much of a history out of him. Is he allergic to any drugs?"

"Not that I can remember."

The ER doctor then prescribed a painkiller containing aspirin, which caused severe internal bleeding and death of the patient. Actually, as it turned out, the family physician's own office records showed that the patient was on anticoagulants prescribed by a specialist; therefore, he should not have been given any drug containing aspirin. This case was also settled out of court.

A few tips: If you're asked for information about a patient by an ER source and you're not sure of the answer, check your office records.

When you're asked to give medical advice to anyone at the ER, have that source repeat back to you what you said. A vital point may get garbled in the translation. Better to straighten it out immediately than to try to straighten it out later in court.

Make a record of all such conversations and place it in the patient's file. It's also a good idea to request a copy of the ER chart for filing.

When the referring doctor and the ER physician differ

Medicine is an art as well as a science, and doctors disagree all the time about modes of treatment. Usually such disagreements are resolved in light of what best suits the patient. However, when the attending physician is in his office and the other doctor is on the phone in the ER, disagreement can have serious legal repercussions.

The ER doctor might say, for example, "The patient seems stable now, but I'm still a bit concerned. Maybe we should hospitalize him."

"What is your concern?"

"I don't know—just a feeling. He doesn't look too good."

"Doctor, I've known this patient for a long time. He never looks too good. Unless you have a sound clinical reason for hospitalizing him, discharge him and tell him to come to my office tomorrow."

There have been times when tomorrow never came for such patients. Some have died shortly after leaving the ER, sparking malpractice suits against both the hospital and the attending doctor.

When an ER patient is transferred to another hospital

This happens occasionally when specialized facilities are needed for proper treatment. Instructions for the transfer are sometimes given by the attending physician, who then goes to the second hospital to take over the care of his patient—only to have trouble finding the patient.

The confusion arises because the attending doctor neglects to notify the second hospital of what's happening. Consequently, when the patient arrives, no one knows who he is or why he's there, and he gets lost in the hospital maze.

This may seem unusual, but believe me, it's not. I know of a number of malpractice actions that have risen from just such incidents.

Play safe. Be sure to make arrangements at both hospitals when ordering an ER patient to be transferred.

Play safe, too, when treating a patient by telephone, the subject of the next chapter.

18

*W*hen treating by phone calls up trouble

*The convenience of a phone can turn into
a legal hazard if you go too far.*

We all know that the telephone is a time-saver. But at what point does the handiness of the telephone become the hazard of legal action?

That's hard to say—individual cases vary considerably—but here's one that lays down some pretty good guidelines. It also shows how high the price of wrongly treating by telephone can be—the case ended in a structured settlement of $8.5 million.

It all started routinely enough in Southern California. A 21-year-old wife, in her first pregnancy, began going to an OBG for prenatal care. There seemed to be no problems, except for a slight rise in blood pressure and a slight albuminuria that developed in the latter phase of pregnancy.

When active labor finally began, the patient's mother took her to a local hospital. They arrived just past midnight. Here's the time sequence of events that followed.

3:30 a.m.: The patient was moved into the hospital labor

room. Only one nurse was on duty, a young woman who had finished her training only a few months earlier.

The patient's blood pressure was high—210/140—and she had edema of the hands and feet. Concerned, the nurse phoned the patient's OBG and asked what she should do. He told her to administer a stat dose of magnesium sulphate, then continue the drug by intravenous drip.

When the nurse hung up, she later testified, she had the "impression" that the physician would come to the hospital immediately. He didn't.

3:30 to 7 a.m.: During this timespan, the nurse said, she phoned the OBG four more times.

Later, in a deposition, the nurse was asked, "During those calls, did you convey [to the doctor] your concern in regard to the [patient's] blood pressure?"

"Yes, I did."

"And can you tell me what his response was?"

"The response was always the same—I'll be in pretty soon."

7 a.m.: Another, more experienced nurse came on duty. After checking the patient, she called the OBG and urged him to come right over. She also notified a hospital anesthesiologist that the patient had gone into a coma and that the internal fetal monitor showed distress. The anesthesiologist inserted an endotracheal tube and had the patient moved to the ICU.

7:45 a.m.: The OBG arrived at the hospital. He and another doctor decided that a caesarean section was necessary to save the patient's life, but the procedure wasn't performed until an hour later.

In his post-op report, the OBG wrote, "By the time the operation started, the patient's pupils were fixed and widely dilated, and the patient clinically was dead, the heart and lungs having just been kept going by the respirator."

The autopsy report identified eclampsia as the cause of death. It stated that the patient suffered toxemia of pregnancy, along with multiple hemorrhages of the liver, brain, pericardium, and interior abdominal wall.

The child, a boy, was delivered alive but with brain damage. Because his father couldn't care for him, the baby was taken in by his maternal grandparents.

There the case might have rested, except for a strange incident that occurred about six months after the birth of the child. A woman, who has never been identified, entered the confessional of a Catholic church in the community and told the priest, "I work in a hospital where I think a wrong has been done. A mother died in birth, and the child was born with defects. I wasn't directly involved, but my conscience is bothering me."

"Why don't you inform the authorities?" the priest asked.

"I'm afraid I'll lose my job. Can you do something?"

The priest then sought out the grandparents of the child and learned they were going heavily in debt to pay the boy's medical expenses.

The matter came to the attention of a Northern California attorney, Frederick C. Michaud, who agreed to take the case on behalf of the grandparents and the child without a fee. He then filed separate malpractice suits against the OBG and the hospital—one for the wrongful death of the patient, the other for damages sustained by the child, now nicknamed Chico. These suits were ultimately consolidated.

The case dragged on for six years. According to attorney Michaud, "The magnitude and complexity of the suit required an extraordinary amount of preparation on our part. Also, the malpractice insurance companies were stonewalling us. They knew they'd have to pay out, and they wanted to put it off as long as possible."

Meanwhile, medical records showed that Chico was having physical problems. For the first six months of his life, he suffered intermittent seizures. At $26\frac{1}{2}$ months, he managed to crawl. At 6, he could walk "in a hesitant, crouched gait" but had a "chronic encephalopathy" that included manifestations of cerebral palsy.

Yet the boy was appealing. As one report stated, "Chico

appears very intelligent. His language skills seem quite good. His personality is pleasant, cooperative, alert, and attentive."

The case was finally settled out of court because, as attorney Michaud puts it, "I felt it was never going to get into court."

The settlement included $750,000 from the OBG specialist's insurance carrier. This was paid into an annuity that, if the boy lives a normal life span, will total about $8.5 million. The hospital settled for a lump sum of $95,000.

Personally, I think the doctor and the hospital got off lightly. If the case had gone to court, Chico himself would have had a tremendous emotional impact on the jury. The award would have been far higher than the settlement.

I'm sure the jury would also have been strongly influenced by the doctor's phone management of the patient. Attorney Michaud pointed that out when he stated, "In general, trying to treat a seriously ill patient by phone is asking for trouble. Even if the physician chooses the right drug, a judge and jury will want to know why he was not concerned enough to come in and titrate the dosage and give hands-on treatment."

Why didn't the OBG come to the hospital when the young nurse on duty first called him?

From the records available, there appears to have been a misunderstanding about the seriousness of the case. The doctor said in a deposition that he wasn't told of the patient's high blood pressure until 6 that morning. He also said the nurse called him only three times, not five, as she claimed.

Three calls were in fact recorded on the nursing chart. The other two, the nurse said, had been noted on the vital-signs sheets. However, when those sheets were requested by attorney Michaud, they could not be found by the hospital.

Also, after a decision to operate had been made by the OBG, a respirator could not immediately be found by hospital assistants. This delayed the surgery.

From what we know of the case, I think we can list these four guidelines to follow in treating by telephone:

1. Consider carefully the competence of the person on the

other end of the line. In this case, the first nurse on duty was inexperienced. Therefore, the OBG would have been wise to contact the nursing supervisor for a clearer report on the patient. The senior nurse might also have been more likely to tell the doctor, "Get in here—this is serious."

2. Consider a possible conflict of interest. Malpractice litigation often pits hospitals and doctors against each other. In fact, at one point in this case, the hospital filed a cross-complaint against the OBG, seeking indemnification from him for any damages it might be assessed. This cross-complaint was later dropped, but it emphasizes the need for a doctor to be on the spot when a possible malpractice situation in which he may be involved arises at a hospital.

3. Consider the need for a written record of what transpires during treatment by telephone. Most doctors keep such a record if they're in their offices, but few do so at home. The doctor in this case had no log of what he said and the hospital nurse said in their various conversations. It's advisable to keep a logbook for such calls conveniently at home, especially by the bedside.

4. Consider the patient's condition, or possible condition. This requires good medical judgment, of course. You don't have to dash off to attend to every nosebleed or stubbed toe that's reported to you, but it's best to be careful when a potentially serious condition arises, such as a patient experiencing troubled labor.

Commenting on this particular type of case, a highly qualified doctor reports, "Severe pre-eclampsia requires on-the-spot, intensive management of fluid and electrolyte imbalance, studies of blood coagulation, fetal monitoring, $MgSO_4$ and antihypertensives. These can hardly be managed by phone—if you expect a good outcome."

In sum, as a physician-lawyer states, "It is axiomatic that a critically ill patient should not be managed by telephone."

It's also wise to be careful about how you bill an ill patient, the subject of the next chapter.

19

The high cost of injudicious billing

When you charge too much or press too hard for payment, you may trigger a lawsuit.

As a professional in a free-enterprise society, you can charge whatever you like for your services. However, if a patient feels you've soaked him far more than the going rate, he's likely to think, "Hey, this guy is making money out of my suffering, so I'll make him suffer." And he looks around for something he can hang a malpractice suit on.

Very often he finds that peg. It may or may not hold up in court, but the point is that the doctor is put through a legal hassle because he charges too much or bills too aggressively. Those two factors, I've found, spark more medical malpractice actions than any other nonclinical cause.

For example, a highly nervous woman underwent open-heart surgery. She was not only concerned about the operation, she was worried because she had no insurance coverage. In view of this, her husband requested the surgeon to hold off any bills until his wife was home and they could deal with the financial aspects of the case.

Nevertheless, while the patient was still recovering from the operation, she received a demand from the doctor's office for a $1,000 "good faith" payment. Greatly distressed, the woman suffered physical disorientation that caused her to be transferred to another hospital, where she died 10 days later.

Her death was attributed to cardiac arrest, which the husband claimed had been brought on by the emotional disturbance caused by the surgeon's imprudent billing. The surgeon's defense was that the bill had been sent out by his office "by mistake and through a misunderstanding of my order not to bill the patient."

His malpractice insurance carrier, however, was uneasy about the emotional elements involved. Rather than allow the case to go to a jury, the carrier induced the doctor to settle for a $12,000 payment.

In another case, a woman contested what she felt were excessive fees charged by a dermatologist.

"Every time I go to him, he performs more procedures than I request, and some are very expensive," she wrote to the grievance committee of the local medical society.

The committee wrote back, suggesting that she discuss the matter with the dermatologist. His response to the woman: "The minute you enter the examining room, and you are on the examining table, you give permission to have me do whatever I deem necessary for your care. That's what is known as implied consent."

The woman disagreed with that and consulted a lawyer about a malpractice suit. Meanwhile, the local medical society urged the dermatologist to return a portion of the $12,500 in fees he had received from the woman. When he did so, the woman dropped her proposed suit. If it had gone to trial, I'm sure that the doctor's "implied consent" claim would have set off an interesting legal debate.

Sometimes an accusation of overcharging brings out something more serious than malpractice—fraud. An example:

An elderly woman underwent six weeks of treatment for a

chronic ailment. She spent two weeks in a hospital and four in a nursing home. Her physician billed her for a total of $8,000. Medicare paid $3,000. The woman had no other insurance.

When the physician hounded her for the remaining $5,000, she appealed to the local medical society. Their investigation disclosed that the physician had charged $60 each for daily visits to the patient for the four weeks she was in the nursing home. Actually, he had visited her there only once. Since charging for medical services that are not delivered constitutes fraud, the evidence was turned over to Medicare authorities for further investigation.

Excessive charges may also bring down on a physician the wrath of his peers. Two instances are reported by Dr. William S. Weil, a past president of the Los Angeles County Medical Association:

• "A burn surgeon spent eight hours in the OR on a case. He charged $23,000. Medicare paid $8,000. Can you imagine a physician charging $23,000 for a procedure? At that rate, his yearly income would be $4.6 million."

• "Another physician saw a patient in a hospital ER, then admitted the patient to the ICU. He charged $200 for the admission, $100 for the ICU visit, and $150 for coming to the ER—a $450 total."

Dr. Weil adds, "Another problem we have with the high cost of health care is some of the surgical fees that are charged for procedures that were once innovative and rare, but are now standard care.

"During all the experimentation and development, the costs were probably justified, but now that they are routine, there has been little or no reduction in the charges. I'm talking particularly about such procedures as colonoscopy, coronary artery bypass, percutaneous transluminal coronary angioplasty, and arthroscopic surgery."

One of the strangest cases of injudicious billing comes from Bruce Walkup, a California plaintiff's attorney. A psychiatrist was treating a female patient in his office several times a week, during which he'd have sexual intercourse with the woman. He'd then bill the husband for the visits.

Eventually the husband found out what was going on and asked Walkup to file a malpractice suit.

"I don't mind his fooling around with my wife," said the husband, "but why is he charging me $50 bucks every time he does it?"

The psychiatrist explained in a deposition, "If I didn't bill for her, my office people would have become suspicious."

The case was settled out of court, and the psychiatrist had to pay the whole sum himself. His insurance carrier refused to cover him because it claimed the malpractice was willful, not involuntary or negligent—a good legal point to keep in mind.

Also keep in mind that a malpractice investigation isn't necessarily bad. It might even be good for you. Read on to find out why.

20

*W*hen it's wise to welcome an investigation

Many doctors instinctively resist a malpractice investigation, but there are times when it's best to cooperate.

In areas of the country where I'm known only by the more sensational aspects of my reputation, I'm sometimes met with suspicion and hostility by the medical community. I well remember one leading physician who said bitterly, "I suppose you're here to get us."

Well, as I explained to him, I'm never out to "get" anyone. Sure, I'm out to get every dollar I can for my client, but only after I've discovered what really happened in the case.

I happen to be a thorough researcher. I also have two excellent investigators who work full time for me. In addition, many of the lawyers on my staff are well-trained and experienced in investigative techniques. So we're usually able to find out everything there is to know about a case. Sometimes that turns out to the advantage of defendant doctors.

The point is that doctors who have nothing to hide in a malpractice situation shouldn't shy away from an investigation.

Two good reasons for this: (1) The person who ducks an investigation looks guilty, whether he is or not. (2) Most plaintiff's attorneys are good investigators, and many have resources that aren't available to doctors to get to the bottom of a case. When those attorneys do get the facts, and they're favorable to the defendant doctor, the case is going to be dropped right then and there.

Consequently, if you're not guilty of malpractice, it's wise to welcome an investigation. Here's a significant instance from one of my own cases:

Two infants were admitted to the neonatal intensive-care unit within a few days of each other at a West Coast hospital. Both were premature, and both were then several days old. Each had an umbilical artery catheter inserted for monitoring and as a route for medication.

The babies were given penicillin and other drugs and were apparently doing well. Then, bluish-black discolorations appeared on the back of each child. Shortly afterward, paralysis set in at the level of T-12, affecting the lower extremities. The cause was unknown.

When it became obvious that the children would be permanently paraplegic, the two sets of parents asked my firm to investigate the tragedy and sue the responsible parties.

By then, the hospital had conducted its own investigation and concluded that the care the babies received had been proper. However, medical experts from a prestigious university advised me that negligence was probably involved. They said the chance of paralysis occurring spontaneously and naturally in two infants at the same time in the same place was prohibitively remote. So they concluded that there had to be some on-the-spot cause.

Neither the experts nor the literature, though, could give us any solid clue as to what the cause might be. We went through more than 200 published scientific papers, but all we came up with was speculation.

One paper indicated that paralysis is sometimes a complication of catheterization. Again, the odds of that happening to two infants in the same place at the same time defied probability. We had a real Perry Mason mystery on our hands.

When I eventually filed suit on behalf of the infants—the youngest plaintiffs I've ever represented—I named the hospital, two attending doctors, three medical consultants, and various John Does. Ordinarily, I don't like to use the "shotgun" approach, but this time it was necessary. Nobody wanted to open up the records or provide information voluntarily.

The hospital was in a particularly embarrassing position. Another baby had died there under strange circumstances at about the same time as the incident involving the two infants. To complicate matters, the hospital was coming out with a new bond issue and didn't want any further adverse publicity.

As usual, doctors were the first to come under suspicion. Also as usual in cases of this sort, there was a certain tension between the medical staff and the hospital administration. Each side pointed fingers at the other.

Our chief investigator was Morris Beatus, a highly capable young lawyer, who's well-versed in medico-legal matters. Beatus is adept at creating rapport with doctors. He understands their problems and apprehension. He soon had their cooperation in trying to solve the strange case of the paralyzed babies. Nurses and pharmacologists also helped Beatus search for errors or accidents.

This clinical detective work was interrupted by rumors that ran through the semirural community—tales of a psychopathic "baby killer" at large in the hospital. The chance that the babies had been deliberately harmed by a deranged person was remote, but the possibility had to be checked out.

Everyone who'd been near the children in the neonatal unit was investigated, including visitors. No one, it appeared, had an opportunity to do harm, since other persons were always present.

However, this left the disquieting possibility that harm could have been done by two or more people working together in some insane conspiracy. This, too, was checked out, but no substantial evidence could be found to support the theory. Still, it contributed to the air of anxiety in the hospital.

Most leads went nowhere. Records showed that the medications given to the infants were appropriate and the dosages proper. The catheters had been correctly inserted and maintained. And no fault could be found with the nursing and monitoring procedures—at least as far as the hospital charts indicated. Just about everything that could have induced paralysis was ruled out.

It was a baffling and frustrating experience, but at least it had one positive result. As several physicians passed one of our investigators in the hospital corridor, a doctor called out, only half facetiously, "Well, have you enough to hang us yet?"

"No," responded the investigator, "but we do have enough to slip your heads out of the noose."

That was true. The records and our investigation clearly showed that the doctors involved had done everything right. They had closely attended to the infants, rendered them high-quality care, and fully recorded events as they occurred.

Furthermore, when the physicians had first observed the paralysis, they immediately contacted medical experts at several top universities for assistance. They had also called in some local specialists for consultations. In short, the doctors had done all they possibly could. We promptly dropped them from the suit.

Beatus persisted with his investigation. Ironically, when all possibilities had been narrowed to one, we were faced with another dilemma: We appeared to have a solution to the mystery, but could we use it in law?

At that point, I called a staff conference. Beatus explained the situation: "Hospital records show that correct dosages of medication were given to the infants. But were those recorded dosages actually received by the babies? And were the medications free of contamination?"

Beatus elaborated: "In going over the hospital, I found a

small refrigerator on the floor between the neonatal and adult coronary-care units. Penicillin was temporarily stored there until it was needed in either unit. Thus, some of the penicillin was in adult-dosage vials. The infants probably received either bad penicillin or an adult dosage—or perhaps both. Unfortunately, we don't have any hard evidence to prove it."

"Why not?" I asked.

"Because when the vials of penicillin were being taken from the refrigerator to the lab for study during the hospital's investigation, they were dropped. The contents were lost, and the broken vials were discarded."

"Why didn't we learn about this sooner?" I asked.

"No record was made of the incident. I learned of it only after taking depositions from the hospital staff."

"Do you think they were deliberately dropped?"

"I don't know. I was told it was an accident, and I don't see how we could say otherwise on the evidence we have."

We couldn't, but we had a way around the problem. In law, if key evidence is lost—either innocently or deliberately—that information can be brought to the attention of a judge and jury. This was the basis of our case against the hospital. All indications, we claimed, pointed toward either bad penicillin or an overdose of the medication, or both, constituting gross negligence.

The hospital fought that claim right up to the courthouse steps. By then, the paraplegic children were 4 years old. I was determined to do all I could for them. My preparation for their day in court included a large color illustration, showing exactly how a tiny body would react if given too much or impure penicillin.

I never got a chance to use that illustration. On the eve of the trial, the hospital lawyers agreed to a structured settlement. The terms for each child included $550,000 to be paid at once, $750,000 to be paid in installments, and an annuity of $25,000 to be increased 4 percent per year for life. The total payout for each child could reach $26 million.

That's one of the largest awards or settlements my firm has ever won for a medical client. For me, it's also the most personally satisfying because I was able to help those children.

21

Can a private eye help you to win your case?

Sometimes—but only if you choose the right individual; the wrong one may make a shambles of your case.

When I was a young attorney, I knew a private investigator who used a crude but effective ploy for flushing out plaintiffs who were faking disability. He'd deposit fresh dog droppings on the front steps of the claimant's home in the darkness just before dawn, then sit in his car and wait for developments. They usually weren't very long in coming.

Example: A rather prissy bookkeeper, who claimed to have suffered back and leg injuries, came hobbling out with a cane to pick up the morning paper. Spotting the dog deposits, he popped back in the house, discarded his cane, and came back with a broom to briskly whisk away the unwelcome doorstep decorations.

Result: The investigator snapped photos of the activity, and the bookkeeper ended up in the loss column as far as his claim was concerned.

Private eyes today are still effective in ferreting out false claims of injury, although through more sophisticated means than dog droppings and snapshots. Some private investigators even specialize in medico-legal cases, and in general they do a good job. On the other hand, ordinary private investigators may be insensitive to the professional issues involved in medical malpractice cases. Consider the following two cases, as reported by James Griffith, a top malpractice defense attorney based in Philadelphia.

Case number one, which worked out great: "The slickest PI I ever met was a detective hired by a doctor's lawyer to check out a patient with a seven-figure, impotence-after-surgery claim. I represented the insurer in the case. There definitely was some liability on the doctor's part. During a sterilization procedure, the man's genitals had been burned when an electrocautery spark set fire to the alcohol in the sterilization solution. But was he really impotent or just planning to exploit the accident?

"The couple lived in an apartment. The PI posted a notice in the laundry room that the Kinsey report was being updated and that the help of tenants in this important scientific project would be most appreciated. He visited tenants on the first floor, then stayed away a week, figuring the women who'd been interviewed would be telling their friends.

"He worked the second floor, waited another week, and then went to his real target in her third-floor apartment: the plaintiff's wife. By this time, she was feeling overlooked and dying to be interviewed. She bragged that her husband was a world-beater who even rushed home from work at lunchtime on some days for matinee performances.

"The PI played dumb. 'Gee,' he said, 'you and your husband have such an incredible sex life that my people are liable to think I made this one up. Would you mind signing my case report so my colleagues won't challenge me?'

"When the case went to trial, the doctor's attorney waited

until the patient's wife was almost finished with her tearful testimony about her hubby's impotence. Then his associate walked into the courtroom with the private investigator. The woman discontinued her testimony, gulped, and said, 'I want to talk to my attorney privately.'

"The judge gaveled a recess, and after a short conference, the patient's attorney stepped up to the bench and told the judge his clients had rethought their position and decided to accept the insurance company's offer to settle."

Case number two, which could have been a disaster: "One of my physician clients asked me to retain a private eye to verify or discredit a young woman's contention that her back injury was iatrogenic. I'd used this PI for routine investigations, and I assumed he'd simply find out who her boyfriends were and perhaps determine the current condition of her back through them.

"Unfortunately, he liked her looks. He tailed her, picked her up in a bar, took her home, and had a wonderful time. Then he came to my office the next day with a big fat grin on his face to tell me he could personally testify beyond a shadow of a doubt that there wasn't a thing wrong with her back.

"'You dumb S.O.B.!' I said. 'You walk into the courtroom with me, she takes one look, stands up, screams rape, and you, I, and my doctor's case go down the tube together.'"

I personally know about another case that had a similar end. A doctor hired a beautiful call girl to seduce a former patient who claimed to be impotent. The gal carried off the seduction in fine fashion, but the doctor's attorney had a fit when he heard about it.

"That's entrapment and harassment," he told the doctor. "If you use that evidence, you could land in a lot of legal trouble. Forget it."

Movie cameras are often used by private eyes to obtain evidence. In an Arizona case, a truck driver claimed he'd been disabled from the waist down after back surgery. However, a

PI who discreetly followed the trucker around with a movie camera obtained some excellent footage of him nimbly climbing all over his huge rig.

After the movie was shown in court, the jury found in favor of the defendant doctor.

The evidence in a California case was even more convincing. The plaintiff claimed he couldn't walk or bend over because a surgeon had disabled one of his knees. A private investigator kept watch on the man's house for several days, but with no luck.

The PI was about to give up when the plaintiff appeared one evening with his wife. They began washing the family car in the driveway, which was on a slope. Accidentally, the wife released the emergency brake, and the PI got graphic shots of the plaintiff holding back the 4,000-pound car, taking most of the weight on his supposedly bad leg.

The doctor won the case.

Another doctor didn't choose his private investigator well. This PI parked his car so close to the plaintiff's house and acted so suspiciously that neighbors called the police. A newspaper reporter who heard the police call followed the patrol car and wrote a humorous feature about the bumbling private eye. The doctor who'd hired him didn't laugh.

In sum, a private investigator *can* help you to win a malpractice case, but use good judgment. Three tips:

1. Do you really need a PI? Put that question to your attorney. If he says, "No," or even, "Probably not," don't hire one. The indiscriminate use of a PI sometimes reflects what others might construe as desperation, even underhandedness.

2. Never retain a private investigator yourself—have your lawyer do it. He probably knows more than you about the right type of PI to bring in.

3. Make sure your lawyer keeps you informed about what the PI is doing. Key questions to ask the lawyer: Do the methods used infringe on anyone's civil rights, or on laws against secretly recorded conversations? Do they constitute entrapment or harassment? Will the evidence prove the plaintiff is a liar, or merely turn a jury against you for "spying."

If the answers are all satisfactory, a private investigator is probably worth a try.

Selecting the right lawyer to represent you in a malpractice suit is even more important than selecting a private eye, as we'll see in the next chapter.

22

*P*icking the right lawyer

Whether you retain a defense attorney yourself, or your insurance carrier assigns one, check him thoroughly. Here's how.

One of the most frequent complaints I hear from doctors who lose malpractice cases is, "I had a lousy lawyer."

More often than not, the lawyer isn't all that bad—simply the *wrong sort* of lawyer. You wouldn't send a patient with a double hip fracture to a dermatologist, yet many malpractice defendants go to trial with lawyers who are general practitioners, or who specialize in real estate, or divorce law, or something similar. You should watch for these points:

1. Don't entrust your malpractice defense to anyone other than a skilled trial lawyer with a good track record in medico-legal matters.

2. If a lawyer is assigned to you by your malpractice insurance carrier, don't assume he's the right attorney for you. He may, in fact, be all wrong. Also, you don't have to accept him. You can request a replacement.

3. Under certain circumstances, you should retain a lawyer of your own, whether or not you go along with the attorney assigned by your insurance carrier. For example: If the dollar

damages sought by the plaintiff exceed the limits of your coverage, you'd be wise to engage private counsel to defend you
for the excess amount. Several other examples:

• If a hospital is named a codefendant in your suit and
you're both covered by the same insurance carrier, don't
agree to a common defense attorney. There may be a conflict
of interest involved, particularly if there's a difference of opinion between you and the hospital over the case. Try to get the
carrier to assign another lawyer to you—or, failing that, retain
separate representation.

• If a carrier expresses doubt about whether it's obliged to
defend you, bring in your own attorney immediately and let
him deal with the insurance company. Some carriers nitpick
about technicalities, such as reporting a malpractice claim
within a certain time limit. They just might hoodwink a doctor
into thinking he's lost his right to coverage, but they'll have far
less luck with a lawyer.

And, incidentally, even if the carrier agrees to defend you,
have your own attorney monitor the case.

As far as selecting the right attorney is concerned, here's a
four-part quiz that will help you to decide:

1. Do you feel comfortable with your lawyer?

We all know that patients respond best to treatment when
they feel compatible with their doctors. It's the same with the
lawyer-client relationship. You have to feel you can confide in
your lawyer, trust him, and work well with him. It's a sort of
partnership.

If the lawyer doesn't listen to you, doesn't seem to respect
your opinions, doesn't invite any input from you, then it's not
a partnership—it's a one-man deal. Look for a lawyer who re-
alizes the importance of teamwork.

2. Does he make you feel guilty?

I once knew a lawyer called "Gloomy Gus" who automatically
figured everybody was on the wrong side of the law. His first

question to a client would be, "All right, what did you do to land in this mess?" His skeptical attitude clearly indicated that the "mess" was all of the client's making.

Now, healthy skepticism is fine—just about all good trial lawyers have it—but when it extends to downright pessimism, that's unhealthy. It's also contagious, and it can affect you. You might lose heart, give up, and lose the case.

Therefore, if a lawyer starts shaking his head glumly before he's even heard all the facts of your case, be cautious. Defending a malpractice suit is depressing enough in itself—you don't need a Gloomy Gus to add to the dark clouds.

3. Can you talk to him?

Busy lawyers are like busy doctors—you can't always get hold of them when you want. Even when you do, they may not have the time or inclination to listen properly.

These busy-busy fellows usually fly warning signs right at the beginning. They schedule meetings, then put them off, often with the excuse of more pressing business.

To you, no business is more pressing than your own. Get a lawyer who's able and willing to set aside sufficient time to deal with your concerns, who listens to you conscientiously, and who's reasonably available when you need him.

4. Is he competent?

Try out a few forensic medical terms on him. If he doesn't know what you're talking about, he's not an experienced medical malpractice lawyer.

Also be wary of the fellow who urges you right off to settle the suit in your own "interests." He just might be looking out for his own interests. If the case is tough, he may not feel competent enough to carry it successfully through trial. By inducing you to settle, he's getting himself off the hook.

You, however, would be left with a barb or two or three in you. A settlement blots your record, it takes away from you the right to countersue the plaintiff, and it leaves you vulnerable to a hike in your malpractice premium, maybe even cancellation of the policy.

One last note of advice: Decide well before going to trial whether or not your attorney is deficient. After that, you may find that you've put your fate into the hands of a loser.

You may also be tempting fate if you resist a deposition. Read on to find out why.

23

A *good way to win without going to court*

Properly handled, a deposition can work well enough to have the case against you dropped.

Here's a tale of two doctors who were sued separately for malpractice. Both had equally good grounds for a solid defense. One, however, prolonged his case, while the other managed to cut it short.

When the first doctor received a subpoena to appear for a deposition, he ignored it. Later, he got tough with his own lawyer, who was pressing him to show up for the deposition.

"I'm too busy to appear," the doctor declared, "and I'm not going to appear. The charges against me are ridiculous—they'll be thrown out of court, anyway."

The doctor himself was subsequently haled *into* court for contempt. The judge fined him and gave him a lecture on the legal consequences of ignoring a subpoena.

Although the doctor then appeared at the deposition, he

was unprepared and uncooperative. He dodged questions, or gave grudging and even contemptuous answers.

Years later, when the case went to trial, those answers came back to haunt the doctor. The plaintiff's attorney used them repeatedly to make the physician look callous or indifferent.

The doctor eventually won the decision, but it was a rough battle all the way—and he didn't come out entirely a winner. His insurance carrier cancelled the policy because of his uncooperative manner.

On the other hand, the second doctor came to his deposition promptly and well prepared. He not only answered questions fully and effectively, he testified so strongly that the case against him was dropped. The plaintiff's attorney knew it was useless to go to court.

Moral: You should welcome a deposition. It's sort of a pretrial audition of whether or not you'll go to court. If you perform well, and if you have a good case, you might not have to travel the long, rocky road to and through a trial.

A deposition—also known as an examination before trial—is a hearing of facts and arguments that both sides intend to present in court. That's the stated purpose. The unstated purpose of the plaintiff's side is to make you look and sound like a lousy, uncaring physician who inflicted damages on a patient. Never lose sight of that fact when testifying at a deposition.

A problem for some doctors is that they don't take a deposition seriously enough. It's usually held in an attorney's office, far removed from the majestic trappings of a courthouse. There's no judge. Lawyers for both sides are on hand. The only other person required to be present is a stenographer, who records everything. You are under oath, and you may be subjected to both direct and cross-examination.

Otherwise, the atmosphere is informal. The attorneys may even engage in some banter.

Don't enter into it. Anything you say in a deposition can be repeated in court. In one instance, a doctor made what he intended to be a friendly, ethnic joke about his own attorney.

The plaintiff's lawyer later read that portion of the deposition to the jurors, some of whom were members of that ethnic group. They weren't amused. Other guidelines:

Don't lower your guard

Some trial lawyers assign junior members of their firms to handle depositions. That works out all right in some cases, but it can have a detrimental effect on a doctor-defendant. He might figure, "Well, my lawyer apparently doesn't figure this is important, so why should I?"

Result: The doctor is lulled into a false sense of security at a time when he should be alert. Your career may be on the line, so don't accept second-rate representation at a deposition. Insist on a lawyer of your choice.

You can also insist on setting the deposition at a time that's convenient for you. These hearings don't have to fit into a court calendar—they can be adjusted to accommodate those involved. Just ask your lawyer to make the adjustments. Don't ask it too often, though—it can backfire on you when an angry plaintiff's lawyer finally gets you on the hot seat.

You also have to be wary of the attorney who plays it cool and casual, even seemingly concerned for your welfare. Words to watch out for:

"Thank you for coming, Doctor. I'm sorry to put you through all this." You'll be the one who's sorry if you believe he's really sorry.

"I'm delighted to meet you, Doctor. I've heard a lot about you." Translation: He's heard a lot about you from the plaintiff, and it's all bad. He's buttering you up for the grill.

"Now, let's just relax, Doctor. Take off your jacket and have a cup of coffee." Have the cup of coffee if you want, but don't relax—not unless you want to become a sitting duck in a shooting gallery.

"I'm sure we can work all this out, Doctor. My client isn't unreasonable in her request for damages." You're not going to agree with that if the plaintiff is asking for Fort Knox, but you just might lower your guard a little if you're led to believe you can settle quickly for a few thousand. Keep your defense up. The plaintiff's side can raise the amount of damages sought as soon as they get the information they want out of you.

Don't be intimidated

The judicial system is basically trial by combat. That means you have to be prepared for a certain amount of psychological warfare.

When you arrive at the attorney's conference room for the deposition, for example, you may be confronted by walls covered with certificates bearing witness to the lawyer's academic and professional achievements. There might even be blow-ups of favorable news reports about him, along with multi-million-dollar checks he's received in malpractice awards. You may feel unnerved, but don't show it. Keep your composure, sit down, and make yourself comfortable.

If the plaintiff's attorney is the aggressive type, he'll probably come on strong right at the beginning. A favorite ploy is to put down the defendant-doctor.

"In your own office," he may say sternly, "you're the boss. The law is the boss here."

Or he might start quoting from leading medical authorities in the defendant-doctor's field, intimating that they'll be called as expert witnesses. Don't be bluffed. Chances are the attorney has simply picked up a few phrases from the authorities' written works. And even if the authorities have agreed to appear, your lawyer can depose them in advance of the trial and find out exactly what they intend to say.

Be prepared for intensive questioning on your background. The plaintiff's attorney may even insinuate that he knows of dark secrets in your past. If there are any blots on your record, don't deny them. That would be a fatal mistake, branding you at the start as a liar.

The truth, of course, is your best defense, not only at the deposition but throughout the case.

Don't be misled

Before going to the deposition, review the medical records in the case, then take copies along with you. Be particularly alert when the plaintiff's attorney prefaces a question with, "Now, just off the top of your head, Doctor—" or, "I'm sure you have a good memory, Doctor, so...."

Whether you have a good memory or not, don't let the attorney lead you into one of the most harmful of all deposition traps—commenting on something about which you're not sure. If you have any doubt at all about a question, simply say, "I'd like to check the patient's chart to refresh my memory."

At a trial, it's not advisable to keep looking to the record. That could have an adverse impact on the judge and jury. But at a deposition, you can—and should—check the chart as much as you feel is necessary. Don't speculate.

Similarly, if you're confronted with records you've never seen before—say, of an autopsy—and asked to comment, decline to do so until you've had sufficient time to study them.

Finally, don't be misled by the lawyer who ends each phase of his questioning by asking, "Now, are you sure that's all you have to say on this subject?"

You'll be tempted to cut the deposition short simply by saying Yes. Don't. Say, "That's all I can think of right now."

This leaves you an opening to elaborate on the topic later at the trial. If you respond with a flat Yes, then come up with additional testimony on that subject at the trial, you could be hit with a charge of withholding evidence.

Don't wear yourself out

There's an old Latin saying that roughly translates as, "Don't let the bastards wear you down." I would never, of course, refer to any of my esteemed colleagues in law as illegitimate offspring, but there are some who are quite skilled at dragging out a deposition—up to 10 hours or so on occasion.

Be prepared for that. Try not to come to the deposition in a fatigued condition. Pace yourself on the stand as you would in a long-distance run. Don't burn yourself out with indignation over what you feel are insulting or harassing questions.

Most important of all, don't become bored with repeated queries that sound alike. The purpose here is to get you to contradict yourself. If you do that, the opposition can label you a liar in court.

Of course, at all times during the deposition, your attorney will be on hand to challenge unfair or inadmissible questions by the plaintiff's lawyer. Even so, it's best to know in advance where the pitfalls are. Also try to have your attorney arrange a limit on the length of the deposition—say four or five hours.

One last tip: Be sure to study a transcript of the deposition before going to court. The trial may not occur until four or five years after the deposition, and something in it may conflict with your present situation or medical thinking. If so, be certain you can explain the conflict.

Even when the time gap is relatively short, conditions can change drastically between a deposition and a trial. I once represented an attractive woman whose husband had been killed in a car crash. My plan was to present her as an inconsolably bereaved widow.

The case came to trial more than a year later. When I saw the widow two days before we were due to go to court, I grabbed a phone and began to negotiate a settlement. The "bereaved" widow was so pregnant that she might have produced an offspring on the witness stand.

Even if the deposition doesn't get you off the hook, it's a good way to prepare for trial. There are also many other ways to do that, and we'll explore them in the next chapter.

24

The right way to prepare for trial

Proper consultation with your lawyer is a must, but many other things can ease the ordeal and help your chances of winning.

I was once cross-examining a doctor-defendant in a malpractice case who had testified very competently under direct examination by his attorney. As I questioned him, however, he became more and more uncertain, falling back on generalities or such responses as, "I don't know," or, "I'm not sure."

Finally, I said, "Doctor, why can't you be more specific?"

"Because," he blurted, "my lawyer didn't tell me you'd be asking questions like these."

Well, his lawyer *should* have told the doctor the kinds of questions I'd be asking. To prepare properly for trial, you not only have to know what your side is doing, you also have to anticipate what the other side will do.

Insist that your attorney review with you every aspect of the case, including all pertinent medical and financial records, memos, and letters. Then have him fill you in on what you'll do and say in court.

Don't hesitate to make suggestions yourself, especially
about medical matters—even the pronunciation of clinical
terms. I've seen more than a few attorneys weaken their arguments by mispronouncing medical phrases and words. As a
juror once remarked to me, "If he got that wrong, what else
did he get wrong?"

Don't hold back from your attorney anything that's unfavorable to you. If he knows in advance, he can shore up weak
spots in your defense. If he doesn't know, both he and you will
be in for a nasty surprise when the truth comes out in court.

Keep in mind that from the moment a malpractice suit is
filed, you'll be the target of intensive investigation by the
plaintiff's side. If there's a smudge on your record anywhere,
it will probably come to light.

Also keep in mind that any information you give your attorney is privileged. Don't be reluctant to tell all.

If you find anything in the medical record of the case that
reflects badly on you, don't try to edit it to make yourself look
good. Such tampering can be disastrous.

One doctor, in changing the chronology of events, put
down a treatment date of February 29. In court, the plaintiff's
attorney scathingly demanded of the doctor how he was able
to find such a date in what was not a leap year.

Bear in mind that some malpractice carriers cancel coverage if the doctor-defendant talks to the plaintiff's lawyer. Even
if there's no such clause in your policy, it's unwise to speak to
the enemy, though you may be tempted.

For instance, the plaintiff's attorney might call and say
something like, "Doctor, I hate to put you through all this.
Why don't we just get together and talk it over. I'm sure we
can work something out."

That's the friendly approach. Don't give in to it. Probably
all the attorney wants is information he can use against you.
Refer him to your attorney.

Then there's the tough approach. "Doctor," the plaintiff's
lawyer may say, "you don't stand a chance. The facts are all

against you, and a jury will clobber you. Settle now, or I guarantee you'll be sorry."

Don't fold your hand—the lawyer is probably trying to bluff you. His direct and threatening approach may even be unethical. Refer the matter to your own attorney, who may want to pass it along to the bar association's grievance committee.

You might also be tempted to talk to the patient who sued you. Don't. There's nothing to be gained by that once a suit is filed. You may even suffer harm if you say the wrong thing, such as, "I'm sorry," or, "I wish none of this had happened"—comments that could redound against you in court.

It's also unwise to discuss the case with colleagues, assistants in your office or hospital, even your friends or members of the news media—at least, not without first consulting your attorney.

Codefendants are in a special sort of category. Don't figure, "Well, we're all in the same boat, so let's help each other." One or more of the other defendants may, in fact, be trying to get out of the boat and leave you to weather the storm all by yourself.

Let your lawyer handle any joint strategy that's necessary. Talk to the other defendants only as he advises.

Along with mastering the facts of your particular case, read key text books and the literature on the medical problem involved. Jot down anything that might help you, and pass these notes along to your attorney. Make sure that he, in turn, researches cases similar to yours. Legal precedents may have been set that will strengthen your defense.

Consider with your lawyer basic questions and answers that probably will be involved in your testimony. Style as well as substance is important here. Tape-record your responses to anticipated questions, so you can spot any speech mannerisms that detract from the impact of your testimony.

Do you hesitate? Do you slur your words? Do you sound as though you're evading the question? Do you stray from the facts? Do you bring in irrelevant matters? Do you sound verbose? If the answer to any of these questions is Yes, correct the defect.

Remember the courtroom is a stage, where appearances are critical. It's not enough to tell the truth—it's important to act and sound as though you're telling the truth. It all contributes to credibility.

If possible, attend a malpractice trial. Familiarize yourself with the courtroom, follow the sequence of events, notice carefully who does what, particularly the doctor-defendant. Put yourself in his place, watch how he acts or reacts. If he appears to be ineffective, note what he does or says wrong so you can avoid his drawbacks. On the other hand, if he comes through as a strong and convincing witness, study and emulate his strengths.

Before going to court in your own case, find out from your attorney all you can about the opposing lawyer. What can you expect from him? Is he tough? Is he sly? Is he intimidating?

When you know what to anticipate, you'll be more likely to cope with the particular style of your opponent.

Also prepare for what the opposition's strategy might be. Have your attorney act as a devil's advocate and ask you questions that the plaintiff's lawyer is likely to put to you.

Don't fear there's anything illegal or unethical about this sort of preparation for your courtroom appearance. There's not, but many plaintiff's lawyers play on this fear.

"Did you discuss this case with your attorney?" they'll demand threateningly.

Sometimes a doctor-defendant verbally dodges so much that jurors begin to think, "He must be guilty of *something.*"

Here's the correct line of response:

"Did you talk to your lawyer about this case?"

"Yes."

"What did he tell you?"

"He told me to tell the truth."

Finally, be prepared to play the postponement game. As the trial nears, and your tension mounts, the plaintiff's attorney might put off the starting date—not once or twice, but repeatedly. As a result, your professional and private lives may be disrupted, your nerves may be frayed, and your patience may be exhausted—so much so that you're ready to give in and settle.

Try not to surrender. Repeated postponement of trial by a plaintiff's lawyer usually means he doesn't have much of a case—and you do. Always play out a winning hand.

Also don't overlook any good bets for your defense, such as the one I'll explain in the next chapter.

25

A good line of defense that's sometimes overlooked

It's called contributory negligence, and it's very effective against plaintiffs who are themselves at fault.

In a malpractice trial, a strong offense is often the best defense. In a Georgia case, for example, a truck driver sued a thoracic surgeon for "botching" a rib resection, causing paralysis of the right arm, side, and shoulder. Evidence introduced at the start of the trial showed that the surgeon had indeed damaged a muscle controlling the right scapula.

Fortunately for the surgeon, he had a lawyer who knew how to play a legal trump card aggressively. Without denying that damage had occurred, the attorney quickly brought out two pertinent facts: (1) The patient had failed to follow the surgeon's instruction to exercise the arm and shoulder. (2) The patient had neglected to take medication as prescribed.

The defense attorney then rammed home his main point: The injury originally caused by the surgeon was minor and had little effect on the patient's shoulder. If the patient had performed the exercises and taken the medication prescribed by the surgeon, he would not have become paralyzed.

Two medical experts backed up this contention, and the jury found in favor of the surgeon. The decision was upheld on appeal.

The line of defense effectively used here is "contributory negligence," meaning that damage sustained by a plaintiff is due to his or her own conduct. It's a good line of defense, and I'm surprised it's not brought into play more often.

The fault lies somewhere between the doctor-defendant and the defense attorney. The doctor fails to tell all that the plaintiff did and didn't do, and the lawyer neglects to ask.

Defense attorney Jack E. Horsley tells a marvelous story of how the impact of contributory negligence came forcefully to his attention when he was just starting out in practice. A small-town GP had been accused of malpractice, and Jack was assigned to defend him. The plaintiff was a plumber who claimed the doctor had treated a back ailment improperly, causing permanent injury.

"When the GP and I got together for our first conference," Jack relates, "I questioned him learnedly and at length about such matters as 'due care' and 'local standards of practice.' He was a crusty, down-to-earth old fellow, who finally cut me off.

"'Young man,' he said impatiently, 'you keep asking me about what *I* did and didn't do. Why don't you ask me about what that damn-fool plumber did and didn't do?'

"'All right,' I said, 'tell me.'

"The GP began to tick off the items: 'First of all, he made an appointment and broke it. When he did show up a week later, he was in such a hurry he didn't allow me time to examine him thoroughly. His main concern was to get a painkiller, so I wrote a prescription for one. I also gave him a prescription for a muscle relaxant, but he never even bothered to have that prescription filled.

"'On his next visit, I recommended that he see an osteopath in another town who I thought could help him, but he said he didn't have time to travel back and forth. I suggested that therapeutic exercises might help, and advised him to see the physical therapist at our local hospital. But he didn't do that, either. Now he's walking around with a permanent stoop and blaming me.'

"'Contributory negligence!' I blurted.

"'What?'

"'That's a legal term. It means the patient's own negligence led to the damage.'

"The GP nodded approvingly. 'Now you got the idea, son. Go to work on that.'

"I did, and a judge threw out the suit before it even got to a jury. Since then, in defending doctors and hospitals in hundreds of malpractice suits, I've always been very, very careful to find out exactly what the patient did and didn't do."

That may seem an obvious line to pursue, but some lawyers overlook it. They concentrate too hard on that word "defense." They set up a kind of Maginot Line and wait for the plaintiff's side to attack.

Well, we all know what happened to the Maginot Line— the defense just crumbled. The best legal strategy is to meet the plaintiff's attack with a vigorous counterattack. And the heaviest ammunition for that is evidence of contributory negligence. So if your lawyer doesn't bring up this line of defense, bring it up yourself.

He may demur, saying something like, "Jurors turn against a doctor who tries to blame an injury on a patient."

Don't buy that. It may have been true in days gone by, but not now. In my experience, jurors today are sophisticated enough to weigh evidence against a plaintiff as carefully as they would against a doctor.

A problem crops up, however, when a doctor can't produce records to support a claim of contributory negligence. With no documentation, this defense probably won't hold up.

Moral: Record in the patient's chart everything that he or

she does that's detrimental to good care, such as minimizing symptoms, denying a condition, missing appointments, ignoring medical instructions, failing to take prescribed medication, refusing to go to a hospital, or leaving a hospital against medical advice.

Another problem occurs when a malpractice suit catches a doctor by surprise. He panics or gets flustered, and in his frantic efforts to explain his own possible failings, he neglects to look for the patient's failings and to pass this information along to the defense lawyer.

Moral: In checking the medical record—and your own memory—search for negligence on the part of the patient.

Even if this isn't enough in itself to win the case for you, it might lessen the dollar amount of a jury decision, which is called "comparative negligence." In other words, if the patient has aggravated damage caused by the doctor through some negligence of his own, the jury can scale down the award. Example:

An orthopedist treated an accountant who had suffered a compound fracture of the left os calcis. The wound was debrided, a cast was applied, and two drains were placed in the area of the injury.

Later, when the drains were removed, the patient complained of a bad odor. The orthopedist attributed this to blood that had dried during the healing process.

After discharge from the hospital, the patient returned to his home. A day later, feeling increasing pain, he tried to phone the orthopedist, who was out of his office. A medical assistant advised the patient to go to an ER immediately.

He didn't go, however, until the next day. The cast was then removed, revealing gangrene. To save the patient's life, it was necessary to amputate the leg.

The main question that arose in a subsequent malpractice trial was: When did the infection begin? The answer, according to expert testimony, was when the patient first complained of a bad odor to the surgeon, who should have promptly inspected the wound. The jury awarded the patient-plaintiff damages of $285,000.

That wasn't the end of it, though. The jury also found that the patient himself had been at fault in not going immediately to the hospital ER when so advised. Therefore, the award was reduced by 23 percent, the degree of comparative negligence attributed to the patient.

Along with contributory negligence and comparative negligence, you should get a good perspective on expert medical witnesses, the subject of the following chapter.

26

What you should know about expert medical witnesses

Choosing the wrong one may do more harm than good to your defense.

Expert medical witnesses come in two categories—helpful and hostile. The hostile ones, of course, take the stand against you. The helpful ones are on your side, although they may not be all that helpful in the final analysis.

I remember a case in which I appeared some years ago, representing a patient who'd been left with a shortened leg after an operation. The expert for the doctor-defendant was an orthopedic surgeon who came on strong—a tall and very distinguished-looking physician with extensive credentials and an authoritative manner.

He was a glib talker, too, and I listened carefully as he

reeled off his qualifications, many of them irrelevant to the case. I jotted on a pad in front of me, "This guy is a know-it-all. Give him plenty of room to brag."

Instead of answering the defense attorney's questions directly and concisely, the witness used each one as a takeoff point for a lengthy medical lecture, complete with scientific jargon. Some jurors looked bored—others seemed resentful. Again I scribbled on my pad: "Now he's talking down to us common folk, and some don't like it."

On cross-examination, I said to the witness, "Doctor, I must say you have interesting qualifications. Could we go over them again?"

He was delighted to do so. Occasionally, I stopped him to ask for specifics about a particular credential. Most of them, it soon became obvious, had to do with academic appointments and published writing.

"But, Doctor," I asked, "are you a practicing physician?"

He hedged. "What do you mean by a practicing physician?"

"Well, do you have a medical office and staff? Do you see patients every day? Do you operate regularly?"

He procrastinated further, but eventually he admitted he was not really a practicing physician. Most of his time was taken up with writing and lecturing.

"And I want you to know," he insisted, "that I'm a recognized expert in my field."

That may have been so, but he didn't have the good sense to stick to his field. When I asked him a hypothetical question about headaches that might be associated with an orthopedic operation, he responded with one of his usual lectures.

Having led the witness into the deep waters of neurology, I queried him closely about that complex specialty. It soon became obvious that he was out of his depth.

Floundering, he demanded of me angrily, "Are you trying to imply I'm an incompetent physician?"

"No," I replied, "I'm just trying to assess your capability as an expert witness in this case. You were the one who brought up the word—" I paused for effect, turned to the jury, and concluded, "incompetent."

The defense lost the case, partly because their expert witness had alienated jurors and wrecked his own credibility. Once that was damaged, everything he said was questionable.

Now let me tell you about another expert medical witness I went up against, a mild-mannered cardiologist who didn't appear in the least formidable. He stated his qualifications briefly, emphasizing only that he had been a practicing cardiologist for 25 years.

On the stand, he refused to stray into any other field. When I asked him a question about gastroenterology, he replied, "I don't claim expertise in that area. I'm here as an expert on cardiology."

"But you're an internist," I persisted. "Aren't all internists familiar with both cardiology and gastroenterology?"

"Yes," he responded, "but we don't claim to know all about them. Today, each field is a well-defined subspecialty."

"Well," I went on, "when you graduated from medical school and received your M. D., didn't you think you knew all about medicine?"

"Yes, I did," he answered, but quickly added, "however, that was 30 years ago. Every medical student thinks he knows all about medicine when he graduates."

Several jurors smiled at that reply, and one even nodded in approval.

The witness went on to score more points. His responses to questions were to the point and meaningful. When he used medical terms, he sometimes explained them, but not to the extent of ever talking down to the jury. Despite his low-key manner, he came through as a compassionate, caring person, realistic and objective in his views.

In short, that witness was a good doctor who had brought his bedside manner with him to court, and it worked. His side won the case.

Moral: In helping your lawyer to select an expert medical

witness for your defense, look for a doctor who's not just an ivory-tower specialist, removed from the day-to-day reality of dealing with patients. Also make sure he's not a pompous egotist likely to bore or antagonize jurors. Finally, if possible, find out if he can answer questions directly and precisely, without wandering into fields of practice beyond his expertise.

Other items to consider:

• Does he understand and agree with the medical theory you want to prove in your case? If he doesn't, discard him immediately. At best, he could embarrass you—at worst, he could destroy your defense.

• Will he devote adequate time to your case? Some experts feel all they have to do is appear in court and testify. There's much more to it than that. Your expert has to know all the facts of the case; he should read depositions and participate in discovery procedures himself; he must attend pretrial consultations; and he should be up to date on texts and treatises in his specialty. If he doesn't measure up to all those standards, he's not for you.

• Are you associated too closely with him? I've seen doubt cast on some very good experts by an opposition lawyer who asks right off, "Doctor, are you a friend of the defendant?" If the answer is Yes, jurors will take everything that expert says with a grain of salt. Try to get someone whose association with you isn't too close.

• Is he satisfied with his fee? Most medical experts are paid, and some set a very high monetary value on their expertise. If an insurance company is paying the fee, make sure it's satisfactory with the expert. Otherwise, he may be a reluctant, grudging witness—and those are the worst kind.

So much for *your* expert witness. What about the expert for the opposition? What can you do to minimize the impact of his testimony?

Some suggestions:

• Check the qualifications he claims. I recall an expert medical witness who took the stand and stated he belonged to a long list of prestigious societies. Actually, as an assistant of mine quickly found out by computer, he had membership in only a few of those organizations. On cross-examination, I compelled the expert to admit he had exaggerated his credentials, an admission that wrecked all of his testimony.

• Find out if he's examined the patient. A surprising number of expert medical witnesses don't bother to do this. Once the failing has been established, it should be a simple matter for your attorney to impress on the jury the point that the witness isn't really an expert on the principal factor in the case—the patient.

• Bring out any discrepancies between his training and experience and yours. Just about any M.D. can be called as an expert medical witness. That doesn't mean a jury is going to believe in the expertise of, say, a GP who testifies against a brain surgeon. Nor is the jury likely to go along with contentions of a high-society physician who denounces the standard of care practiced by a ghetto doctor. Help your lawyer to find and make these distinctions.

• Play on his partisanship. Medical expert witnesses are supposed to be impartial—at least, in principle. In fact, they're often extremely biased, particularly where conflicting schools of medical thought are involved.

In situations of this sort, I usually ask the witness, "Doctor, are you sure your school of thought is correct?"

The usual answer is, "Of course."

I then point out that a considerable number of physicians believe in another school of thought, and ask, "What do you think of those doctors?"

I've had some interesting answers, ranging from, "They don't know what they're talking about," all the way to, "They're crackpots!"

Jurors will wonder about a mind as closed as that.

• Test his memory. If an expert medical witness has made a deposition, go through it carefully with your attorney. Then if the witness makes a conflicting statement in court, your lawyer can quickly challenge him. A successful challenge will prompt jurors to think, "Well, if that so-called expert couldn't make up his mind about that issue, what other of his opinions are muddled?"

Expert medical witnesses with faulty memories can be led into other traps. I well remember a case in which Dr. Edgar Gilchrist, a distinguished surgeon, was my expert. The expert opposing us was a highly opinionated physician who kept on denouncing Gilchrist.

I let him go on until cross-examination. I then produced a book written by the opinionated doctor years previously and asked him to read what he had inscribed on the flyleaf.

He did so, but with an extremely reddened face: "To Edgar Gilchrist, my friend and great teacher, without whose world-famed knowledge and surgical skill I would not have been able to produce this book."

That doctor made a mistake in calling my expert a bum, but at least he was honorable in other respects—something that can't always be said about physicians who make a business out of testifying as expert medical witnesses. We'll take a look at them in the next chapter.

27

*H*ow to shut a "hired mouth"

The medical expert who testifies more for pay than principle can be a dangerous adversary—but not if you know how to expose him.

In a Georgia malpractice case a few years ago, a neurosurgeon was accused of injuring a patient by operating too soon in an emergency situation. Damages of $1.5 million were sought, and it looked as though the patient had a good chance of collecting. An out-of-state medical expert for the plaintiff contended that the neurosurgeon should have tried conservative treatment before resorting to the knife.

During the trial, however, the defense attorney came up with a surprise. He introduced evidence that showed the plaintiff's expert had testified previously in another state in a very similar case, and his medical opinion then had been quite different. The expert had said that the defendant-doctor was negligent for *not* performing emergency surgery.

That conflict of opinion was enough for the jurors in the Georgia trial. They returned a verdict that was in favor of the neurosurgeon.

How did the defense lawyer know the medical expert was a man of varying opinions? The lawyer did some simple but very effective research. As soon as he knew he'd be up against an out-of-state expert, he sent an inquiry about him to a large law firm in the witness's home city.

Most big defense firms keep files on expert medical witnesses, especially the gist of their trial testimony and depositions. In this instance, the Georgia defense lawyer received a fat and fruitful package—testimony of the traveling expert in 35 different malpractice cases. That's where the defense attorney unearthed pay dirt—conflicting opinions on emergency surgery.

Medical experts for hire are easily obtainable these days. I run into them all the time at legal conventions, and trial lawyers' publications are filled with their ads. One I recently saw proclaimed, "We can have the right specialist on the stand anywhere in the United States within 72 hours."

I'm not saying that all of these doctors are hacks. Some, in fact, are honest, skilled, and effective—but more than a few are suspect. I know of one attorney who called an agency that represented a certain expert.

"Is he an oral surgeon?" the attorney asked.

"No," was the response, "but if you want him to be an oral surgeon, he'll say he is."

Moral: Thoroughly check the claimed credentials of a medical expert witness. He may not be all he says he is. Once you've showed him up as a liar, of course, he has nothing to say that's credible. Other ways to button up a hired mouth:

• Check on whether the expert is qualified to testify in your area. In a Michigan case, for example, a surgeon was disqualified on two points: (1) The trial court didn't consider him competent to testify as an expert on the applicable standard of care for reading X-rays; (2) He had never practiced in the area where the patient was treated.

In a similar case, in Louisiana, two New York physicians were due to testify as experts. The defendant-doctors objected, claiming that opinion testimony by physicians not licensed to practice in the state was inadmissible. The defendants also contended that they should be held to the knowledge, skill, and standard of care of members in good standing in the medical profession in their own locality.

The trial court reviewed legal decisions in other states, then upheld the defendants' objection. The out-of-state experts were barred from testifying.

Even if an expert claims to be familiar with standards of local medical practice, credibility can sometimes be undercut on cross-examination. Here's part of the transcript of a case in Schenectady, New York.

Defense attorney: "You say you're familiar with our standards of practice. On what do you base that claim?"

Expert: "I've lectured at local hospitals and treated patients referred to me from this area."

"Referred to you by physicians in this area?"

"Yes."

"Name one of those physicians."

"I can't think of one right now."

"Well, we'll give you time. How much time do you need?"

"I don't know. I just can't remember."

"Well, what about those hospitals where you lectured. Name them."

From the expert's response, it was obvious that he'd confused Schenectady with Utica, Syracuse, or some other upstate New York area.

Defense attorney: "It seems that you have a rather poor memory, Doctor."

Expert (weakly smiling, trying to make a joke): "I sometimes have trouble remembering my kids' names."

Nobody laughed.

Defense attorney: "You also seem to be confused, Doctor."

The jury agreed, deciding in favor of the defendant-doctor.

• Find out if your malpractice insurance company keeps track of itinerant medical expert witnesses. Some carriers do, compiling data on plaintiff's experts who are frequently brought into cases all over the country.

Says a senior liability manager for St. Paul Fire and Marine Insurance Company, "While some are dedicated, conscientious types, others seem to be loners or mavericks motivated by personal considerations or financial gain.

"When our claims staff spots the name of a widely traveled expert in a new lawsuit, we alert the attorney in that case to compare notes with the defense attorneys from previous cases. Or if a defense attorney runs up against an unfamiliar expert, he'll contact the St. Paul branch he's working with. The local people fill him in if they can. Otherwise, they contact their liability manager here in the home office, who'll send along whatever information we have about the individual in question."

Similar data might also be obtained through the Defense Research Institute—a 10,000-member outgrowth of the International Association of Insurance Counsel—which is setting up a medical-legal exchange.

"The idea is to cross-index names of medical witnesses with those of member defense lawyers who have encountered them before," explains a DRI official. "Then, if one attorney wants to know about a particular expert, we can say, 'Okay, here are four other members who came up against this guy in the past.'"

• Determine if the expert has broken any laws in your state. This is a long shot, but it can pay off big. In one case, a malpractice defense lawyer became suspicious when he learned that an expert in urology charged $12,000, plus $200 per hour, for testifying.

On checking, the defense attorney found the expert had demanded and received his $12,000 fee *before* he testified, which broke a state law. The expert had also perjured himself by stating he was a board-eligible urologist, which he wasn't. The defendant not only won the case—the plaintiff had to pay all court costs.

In another case, during his deposition, an expert came on very strong against the defendant-doctors. Finally, the defense attorney fired a desperation shot: "Have you ever been convicted of a crime?"

That put the expert on the defensive. "I don't have to answer that," he blustered.

"Well, we'll just stay here until you do," the attorney retorted, and kept hammering at the expert.

In the end the expert admitted he had once been convicted of taking kickbacks in a hospital referral scheme. He didn't appear at the trial of that case, which the defendants won.

Reforms have long been urged in the area of medical expert witnesses. In 1977, the AMA House of Delegates passed a resolution that (1) pressed the courts to refuse to admit as expert testimony the opinions of physicians who don't have clear-cut qualifications as recognized by their peers; (2) condemned those doctors who give misleading testimony or misrepresent their qualifications as expert witnesses; and (3) recommended that state and county medical societies take legal or disciplinary action when physicians testify without having the requisite educational and professional knowledge, testify falsely, or give deliberately misleading testimony.

Dr. Burton L. Wise, of San Francisco, has gone a step further: "I would propose that the system be changed so that the expert be hired by the court as an unbiased witness and that he report to the court. He should be paid by the court, with the costs being borne equally by each side. The court might develop a list of expert witnesses who would be available, with perhaps the help of local and regional specialty societies.

"If this approach were established, it would not necessarily prohibit either side from obtaining its own expert witnesses, but I think that an opinion of an expert retained by the court would carry more weight."

Such reforms may well come about in the future. Meanwhile, if you run up against a hired mouth, you might be comforted by an observation by attorney Donald Fager of the

Medical Liability Mutual Insurance Company of New York:

"In my experience, plaintiffs use the professional witness because the case is totally devoid of merit. We find that plaintiffs can and do obtain testimony from qualified witnesses in cases that are really meritorious."

No matter how well you deal with an expert witness, you'll still get in trouble if you misjudge the judge. We'll see why in the next chapter.

28

Getting along with the judge

This is the most powerful person in the courtroom. Forget that and you can forget about winning.

About 85 percent of the judges in the country are fair, honest, and competent. Among the other 15 percent, you'll find pompous idiots, bigots, bullies, and outright crooks.

So before you get anywhere near the courthouse, ask your attorney what the assigned judge is like. If your attorney doesn't know, he can easily find out. A bad judge is usually well known in the legal community.

Sometimes a lawyer can have an unsatisfactory judge removed from a case, but it's not easy—and the lawyer has to take chances. I remember an instance in Syracuse where the plaintiff's attorney became dissatisfied with the judge's ruling during jury selection.

"Your honor," the attorney finally inquired respectfully, "may I see you in your chamber?"

"Only if it's important," the judge replied.

"It's important."

They then retired to the chamber, where the attorney denounced the judge as being "biased" and "handpicked by the defendants."

In the presence of others, the judge lost his temper and blasted the attorney in rather colorful language, which was exactly what the lawyer wanted. The judge had to disqualify himself for losing his temper. Another judge took over, one who was more to the lawyer's liking.

If a judge displays bias, of course, the case can be appealed. That takes time, though, and can be expensive.

Consequently, whether a judge is fair or foul, treat him with respect during trial. Don't antagonize or provoke him, and *never* question his authority. The judge is kind of a father figure in court, and the jury is part of his family. If he rebukes or reprimands you, the jury may look on that as an offense against the family. That's one reason why the judge is called the "13th juror."

The attorneys in the case are also members of the courtroom family. If you show disrespect for one of the lawyers— either your own or the opposition—you're risking the wrath of the judge. Keep that in mind if you're tempted to let fly at a lawyer who irks you.

The best way to get along with a judge is to come to the witness stand well prepared. Quite often, during the course of your testimony, the judge will interject a question of his own. He wants—and is entitled to get—a correct, straightforward answer.

Unfortunately, as I've observed on occasion, the doctor-witness responds with a surprised look, a suspicious stare, or open hostility. One time I heard a doctor demand of a judge who'd asked a pointed question, "Whose side are you on?"

"I'm not on any side," the judge replied levelly, "I'm impartial. I'm here to help the jury to reach an informed and just decision. I'm also here to maintain order—and you, Doctor, seem to be getting out of order. Now, are you going to answer my question or not?"

The doctor answered it.

Another function of the judge is to keep the trial sailing along on an even keel. Therefore, he may be inclined to look with less than favor on a doctor who disrupts or holds up proceedings, especially one who hedges or rambles.

The ideal way to respond to a question in court is either Yes or No. If some explanation is called for, keep it concise. Don't go into a long discourse.

Also try to refrain from turning to the judge during cross-examination and asking "Do I have to answer that?" Such a query is admissible, of course, but when asked too often, it detracts from the doctor's testimony in two ways: It exasperates the judge, who wants to keep matters moving, and it makes the jury think you're trying to dodge something.

Moreover, your attorney will object if a cross-examiner's question is inadmissible or unfair. Give your attorney time to deal with the issue. Pause before responding to the question. If there's no objection, answer it.

Another surefire way to rile a judge is to appear impatient or in a hurry—failings I've observed in quite a few doctors on the stand. I remember one who took out his watch, scowled at it, then asked the judge, "How much longer will this take?"

"Why?" the judge inquired. "Do you have something more important to do?"

"I have a roomful of patients waiting for me. I'd call that important."

"And in this room, we have justice waiting to be served," the judge retorted. "You'll stay as long as justice demands."

Some doctors go to the other extreme and fawn on the judge. That's not wise. If the judge says something like "Good morning" when you take the stand, respond in kind but don't go any further.

In one instance, the doctor added, "Good to see you, Judge. I believe we have friends in common."

The judge immediately leaned forward and said, "Let's get this straight. Have you ever met me before?"

"No, but—"

"No buts, please. Are you implying that our mutual friends—if indeed we may have any—have spoken to me about this case?"

"No."

"Then let me make it clear that you and I have had no previous association whatsoever, nor have I any reason to be partial toward you in any way. Do you agree with that?"

Witness, meekly: "Yes. Absolutely."

The point here is that the judge and the doctor on the stand are professionals. The judge doesn't want it to appear that two professionals are conspiring against the 12 laymen in the jury box. He has to maintain objectivity.

Two other ways in which trying to curry favor with the judge can get you in trouble:

1. Whispering to the judge, or cupping one hand beside your mouth as you lean toward him and talk to him. This also looks like conspiracy. Don't be surprised if the judge barks, "Speak up! The jury is entitled to hear what you have to say."

2. Speaking to the judge outside of court. If he comes up to you in a courthouse corridor or elsewhere and says, "Hello," it's fine to respond with a similar greeting. On the other hand, it's unwise to approach him. If the two of you are seen chatting together, it might look as if you're in cahoots.

It's also unwise to sound off to others about the judge. There's no law against this, of course, but derogatory observations have a way of carrying back to the judge, who's only human. Your comments aren't going to endear you to him.

Finally, don't get into a squabble with an obviously prejudiced judge. Just keep testifying honestly, courteously, and objectively. The contrast between you and the judge will soon become clear to the jury, and they'll swing to your side.

More about that next.

29

Swaying the jury to your side

Individual jurors may be unpredictable, but as a group, there are ways you can get them to look on you with favor.

In one of the first cases I ever tried, the odds were all against me. Nevertheless, in my summing up to the jury, I gave it everything I had. I argued, I pleaded, I may even have sobbed a bit.

My impassioned performance seemed to have struck a responsive chord in one of the jurors—a motherly little woman who had tears streaming down her cheeks. I figured I had at least her on my side.

When the verdict was rendered, however, the jury was unanimous in its decision against my client.

Perplexed, I sought out the motherly little woman and said, "I thought you sympathized with me. Why were you crying?"

"Because," she replied, "you're so young and you were trying so hard, and I knew I'd have to vote against you."

That's when I first learned about the unpredictability of individual jurors. No one can always foretell what a particular juror is going to do. What you can do, though, is to present yourself in the best possible light to the jury and thus influence their collective judgment. Five ways to do that:

1. Understand your role in the courtroom drama.

Jurors don't want excuses from you—they want medical explanations. Just as they look to the judge for legal guidance, they'll look to you for clinical guidance. Give it to them in an objective, straightforward manner, and you'll be an accepted member of the courtroom team.

Remember, in a medical malpractice case, it's the doctor-defendant himself who most influences the jury verdict.

2. Don't shun the spotlight.

Whether you're sitting at the defense table or on the witness stand, you're always in full view of the jury—literally on stage. Don't get stage fright. Don't cringe or turn your head away from the jury, or stare at the floor or ceiling.

I've heard countless jurors remark of a defendant after a trial, "He couldn't look us in the eye"—a trait that's commonly associated with guilt.

At the defense table, look interested, calm, and confident—but not smug. Don't smirk, roll your eyes heavenward, or shake your head when someone else is testifying.

Don't keep whispering to your attorney during testimony—or pass notes to him unless it's absolutely necessary. This is not only distracting to your attorney—it looks conspiratorial to the jury.

On the witness stand, don't mumble. If a judge has to keep saying "Speak up" to you, jurors may get the impression there's something you don't want them to hear.

Speak clearly and objectively, but don't come through as a cold fish. As a doctor, you'll be expected to have some feeling about the case being tried. Don't be afraid to let concern and warmth show.

Don't address everything you say to the jury. If you're asked a question that calls for a short response, for example, direct your answer to the interrogating lawyer. If you're asked for a medical explanation or elaboration, however, address the jury directly.

This is one of your best opportunities to benefit your own case. Start out by making eye contact with jurors who seem the most interested or sympathetic, but don't overdo it. Don't grin or fawn—don't stare or scowl.

Above all, don't be condescending. Don't talk down to the jurors. Use medical terms when necessary and explain them if necessary, but not in baby-talk fashion. Jurors resent that.

Similarly, don't try to be just one of the boys. Doctors who testify using street talk or sports language are downgrading themselves and their profession. Moreover, jurors don't like being addressed as though they're a bunch of street-corner hoodlums.

In short, talk to the jury as you would to a patient who needs instruction and guidance. Help the jurors to come to a basic understanding of the medical problems involved. In so doing, you'll ally yourself with the jurors, not alienate yourself from them.

3. Be alert to signals the jury might be sending.

There are a lot of jokes about jurors going to sleep during trial, and I've seen it happen more than a few times myself. The snoozing juror is not ordinarily a strong juror, but it may be an indication your testimony is soporific. Try to get some snap in your responses.

Also pay attention to the juror who's gazing at the ceiling, or idly glancing around the courtroom. He's lost interest. Try to bring him back to your concerns. Concentrate on him for a few moments, and try to get across to him that he should be very concerned, too.

If it's soon apparent that he's a lost cause, of course, don't waste any more time on him. Get back to the jurors who *are* interested.

Some may appear interested but impatient. They shake

their heads, they fidget, they drum their fingers on their knees, they twirl pencils, they might even glare at you.

Although that's a classic picture of a hostile juror, don't give up. Often it's simply a juror who's having a hard time making up his mind. Help him by presenting your side more clearly.

4. Don't be vindictive toward the plaintiff.

The main point to keep in mind here is that the jury and the plaintiff—your former patient—have a lot in common. They're laymen; they've all had experiences with physicians; and some of those experiences may have been unpleasant, even disastrous. Therefore, if you belittle or attack the plaintiff, you may in effect be belittling or attacking the members of the jury.

I remember an occasion when an exasperated doctor declared on the witness stand that the plaintiff was "just putting on an act."

The plaintiff, a young woman, was in court, sitting in a wheelchair. Expert medical testimony had shown that she would suffer pain chronically and would never again walk without aid.

I looked at the jurors. Their faces reflected shock and anger, all directed toward the defendant-doctor because of his remark. He lost the case.

I've heard other doctors refer on the stand to the plaintiff as "a moaner and groaner," "a crybaby," or "just a hopeless pessimist." Listening to that sort of comment, jurors are going to think of the doctor as an uncaring practitioner.

Making fun of a plaintiff is risky, too. I recall one doctor who was asked if he'd done all he could for a patient.

"Well," he said, "maybe I should have applied a green poultice."

The plaintiff's lawyer, puzzled, said, "A green poultice?"

"I don't understand, Doctor."

"Forget it. It's a joke."

Nobody on the jury was laughing.

If, in fact, a plaintiff is motivated by avarice, or is stupid or a liar, let your attorney bring that out. Denigrating a former patient is counterproductive for a doctor who professes to be considerate of humanity.

5. Don't doubt a jury's ability to judge medical matters.

A malpractice trial is a minieducation in medicine. The jury listens to expert after expert, doctor after doctor. They absorb what they hear; they fit it into the legal guidance they get from the judge; and they temper it with basic common sense. The result, far more often than not, is a fair and sound decision.

Individually, we may not agree with a decision. I've had cases go against me, and I've cursed or cried in the back of the courthouse. Years later, I've become aware of a point that the jury, in their "lack of wisdom," had perceived at the time of trial, and that I, in my "great wisdom," had missed.

Never underestimate the jury's power of comprehension. It's the greatest means of getting to the truth this side of the confessional.

Of course, jurors need help in getting to that truth, and there's a dramatic way you can give it to them. We'll be more specific about that in the following chapter.

30

The importance of "show-and-tell" testimony

The jury not only hears this evidence but sees it, which gives it double impact.

Many years ago, I became a legal pioneer of sorts by nearly falling flat on my face in front of a jury. I was defending an inmate who was accused of killing another prisoner. The defendant, I contended, had acted in self-defense. The deceased, I declared, was a violent man who was known to carry a knife in prison.

The prosecution pooh-poohed that contention. Where, they demanded, would a man in prison get a knife?

Good question. I passed it along to prison officials, who produced for me a box full of homemade knives that had been confiscated from inmates.

At that time, however, it was difficult to present such evidence in court. Rather than go through a lot of rigamarole, I simply brought the box to court, walked past the jury with it, and sort of stumbled, spilling the knives all over the floor.

The wide-eyed jurors saw for themselves that knives were freely available in the prison, and they agreed with my plea of self-defense.

Since then, I've been dropping not only knives, but medicine bottles, scalpels, pills, forceps, and exploded appendices in bottles into the laps of jurors all over the country. Now, though, the technique is widely used and respectable, especially in medical malpractice cases. It's commonly known as demonstrative evidence. I call it "show-and-tell" testimony.

The purpose is to illustrate, dramatize, and clarify points that may be too complex or technical for jurors to readily grasp. Just about anything visual can be used, but the common props are blackboards, anatomical models, graphs, charts, blown up photos, diagrams, X-rays, tissue specimens, and so on.

Jurors love it because it's entertaining as well as educational. Remember back in medical school when you were sometimes bored by long, dry lectures? Contrast that with the interesting, even electrifying demonstrations you watched of real-life clinical procedures. The difference is to see as well as hear what medicine is all about.

Doctors, I've found, adapt themselves extremely well to demonstrative evidence. By the very nature of their profession, they're teachers—they're used to drawing little sketches to instruct patients on medical problems. It's a simple step to carry that technique into the courtroom.

Don't do it extemporaneously, however. Give some advance thought to what you want to prove and how demonstration can make your points clearer. Pass any ideas you have along to your lawyer and discuss them thoroughly. Above all, make sure your props are going to work.

In one case, for example, a lawyer brought a doorframe into court to show how his client had been injured. When the lawyer tugged at the door, it wouldn't open. He kept tugging at it and muttering to himself until the judge told him, "Give up, Counselor. The door is stuck—and so are you."

In another case, a doctor suggested to me that an anatomi-

cal drawing would help him to emphasize points he intended
to make. I had a drawing made, but the doctor felt it was too
small—it lacked detail and color. We ended up with a banner-
like medical illustration in color that stretched across the
courtroom in front of the jury.

Quite literally, it was enormously successful. The doctor
stood beneath the illustration with a pointer and went through
all of the medical details involved. You could see he was in
close, direct contact with the jury members, and had their full
attention.

A juror told me afterward, "I've never been so fascinated.
That doctor was wonderful."

He was, indeed, but only because he'd carefully planned
and rehearsed his "show" before "telling" about it.

The human skeleton is another effective means of demonstrating a medical condition. In various cases, I've used it to
explain how a sprained ankle can cause a back to ache, how the
nerves are like a telephone line running from one part of the
body to another, sending messages, and how the brain is the
command center of the whole human function.

A note of caution about bringing a skeleton to court: Wrap it
up. The first time I used a skeleton I had to argue with a taxi
driver who objected to the macabre passenger (I had to pay an
extra fare). Later, I had to contend with a policeman who saw
me wrestling my bony friend out of the cab. Finally, as I
lugged my exhibit along the courthouse corridors, heads swiv-
eled all around me and mouths literally dropped open.
There's nothing like a skeleton to attract attention.

X-rays are good, too, especially when they're enlarged.
Comment on the history of a medical procedure also helps. I
once perked up a jury by relating how the Beatles contributed
$500,000 to the development of the CAT scan.

If possible, blow up charts and photos. This adds greatly to
their effectiveness. In one case, I had a hospital record enlarged to 4 feet by 4 feet to show to the jury how erasures had
been made.

Videotape is one of the newest implements of demonstrative evidence. In a famous 1981 case, Chicago attorney John D. Hayes put it to dramatic use. He represented a woman who had entered a hospital for cosmetic rhinoplasty, and came out a spastic quadriplegic.

Hayes used videotape to show how handicapped the plaintiff was. Then, although the woman couldn't talk, he put her on the stand for just one question: "What do you want most?"

Using a word-board, another demonstrative evidence device, the woman spelled out her response: "Stop the pain."

The jury awarded her $9 million—at that time, the highest amount ever awarded in a personal-injury case.

Of all the means of demonstrating medical evidence, the human body is probably the best. Scars, for instance, are frequently exhibited to juries, along with malfunctioning limbs.

Exhibits of a highly personal nature are possible. In a judge's chambers, with the jury present, I was once allowed to bare a woman's breasts and display how terribly they'd been disfigured by inept plastic surgery.

Of course, in a medical malpractice trial, the main point of focus in the courtroom is the defendant-doctor himself, who must explain on the witness stand what he did and why he did it. We'll discuss in the next chapter how that can best be done.

31

How to be a winner on the witness stand

Your testimony can redeem or ruin your medical career. Here's expert advice on the correct things to say and do.

I've been watching doctors testify for more than 50 years, and I'm still surprised by the wide differences in their effectiveness. What does one doctor do that's right? What does another do that's wrong? For some answers, let's go step by step through a trial.

The entry
First of all, don't be late. If you keep the judge and the jury waiting, they're going to remember the times they've cooled their heels and heated their tempers in a doctor's office. That's not going to get you off to a good start.

Be prepared for your call to testify. Don't act flustered or surprised. Gear yourself for the walk ahead of you. I've watched thousands of witnesses on that endless trek to the stand. Many have looked as though they were approaching the electric chair. Some appeared to have lost control of their legs.

Others have glanced wildly about the courtroom, as though seeking escape. One flustered doctor even attempted to shake hands with a surprised court clerk, who was waiting to swear him in.

When things like that happen, jurors wonder why the witness is so panicky and frightened. That's a strike on the doctor before he even takes the stand.

Now, it's natural to be nervous, especially for a first-time witness. Your fear probably stems from a common notion about testifying—that you'll be all alone and highly vulnerable on the stand, surrounded by hostile forces.

Throw that negative idea out of your mind. Your attorney is there to protect you. The judge will keep close watch to see that your rights aren't violated. And the jurors are willing to give your testimony a fair evaluation—*unless* you give them reason to do otherwise.

As you approach the stand, look straight ahead at the clerk who's waiting to administer the oath. Don't mumble your response. Say "I do" in a voice that can be heard by all.

When you're on the stand, don't slump or fidget. Sit up straight, with your back against the chair and your feet firmly on the floor. Settle your hands in a comfortable position. Don't let them wander to your chin, your mouth, your nose, or your hair. I remember one doctor who kept reaching around to scratch his lower back—not a very elegant gesture.

Determine whether there's a microphone on the stand. If there is, position yourself so you can speak into it without squirming.

Wear a conservative suit and make sure your clothes are comfortable. If you're constantly tugging at a tight shirt collar, the jury may think you're struggling with your conscience.

Remember that jurors are patients. Dress for them as you would for patients, not a first-night theater audience. I've seen doctors come to the stand in everything from a velvet tuxedo jacket to a rainbow-hued, custom-made sports jacket. It's not wise to flaunt your affluence in front of jurors who may be making do with their well-worn Sunday best.

Similarly, leave your expensive jewelry at home. Gold cufflinks and a diamond-studded wristwatch are fine, but not when they're flashing in the eyes of jurors.

Incidentally, if your spouse is coming to court—and should, if possible, to show support of you—it's advisable for both of you to wear subdued clothes and no jewelry but your wedding rings. And don't blow a kiss or wink from the witness stand—gestures I've seen a few doctors make.

Be constantly aware of your demeanor. Don't frown, grin, scowl, or grimace. Refrain from such mannerisms as chomping on your eyeglasses or fondling a key ring.

I recall a doctor who actually took out a watch and began to twirl it on its chain, which seemed to dizzy the jury. Their heads revolved in time with the watch—until the judge ordered the doctor to put the distraction away.

The direct examination

For some strange reason that I've never been able to figure out, quite a few doctors get uptight when their own attorneys start questioning them. It may be an underlying feeling that *all* lawyers are enemies. If so, forget it. Your attorney is a friend. Relax and trust him.

Answer his questions concisely. And don't elaborate or embroider. If more detail is needed, he'll ask for it. A dialogue is more informative for the jury—and much more interesting to listen to—than a monologue.

Cite only credentials that show your competence as a doctor. If you go on and on about how you belong to this great civic organization or that prestigious club, you'll not only lose the jury, you'll come through as conceited and a blowhard.

Don't rely too often on such responses as, "I don't recall," or, "I don't remember." As the most important witness in your own case, you're expected to know pertinent facts and dates. Otherwise, you'll sound evasive or stupid.

However, if you truly don't know the answer to a question,

don't guess at it. Simply say, "I'm sorry, but I don't know." This will enhance your credibility and stave off an attack by the opposition lawyer, who *will* know the answer that you guessed at.

In one case, a doctor tried to excuse a wrong response by saying, "It was an educated guess." This gave the opposing lawyer an opportunity to retort, "Doctor, you obviously need re-educating."

It's acceptable, of course, to refer to records to refresh your memory, but don't overdo it. One doctor lugged a whole file-box of notes with him to the stand and clung to it as he would to a lifebelt. No matter what his attorney asked him—even a question as simple as, "Doctor, what is your name?"—he pawed through the records.

He exasperated not only the judge and jury but also his own attorney, who ripped the filebox away from him and plunked it on the defense table.

At least that doctor brought his records to the stand neatly boxed. I've seen other doctors produce ill-assorted papers from shopping bags, suitcases, and bowling-ball carriers. If you're disorderly with your recods, a jury just might surmise that you're sloppy in other aspects of your practice.

Moreover, if you bring papers to the stand, make sure there's nothing in them that can damage your testimony. The papers become part of the evidence, and the opposition lawyer can examine, comment on them, or even read from them.

For example, a doctor consulted his personal diary on the stand to verify certain dates. The plaintiff's attorney then glanced through the diary and made such comments as, "I see you have a lot of golf dates, Doctor," and, "You spend a lot of time with your financial adviser, don't you?"

Beware of citing a book or its author as "authoritative." Once you get into a book, the other side can get into it, too, and there's never been a book written that doesn't have some contradictory language.

Be absolutely honest on the stand. Any hint of prevarication will kill you instantly with the jury. Complete candor will win you points.

In one recent malpractice trial, the doctor admitted at the outset, "I made a medical mistake." Indeed he had, but it was not negligence, and the jury came to realize that was true, largely because of his forthright approach. They returned a verdict in his favor.

Contrast that with another case in which a surgeon denied that an operation he'd performed had weakened and deformed a patient's leg.

"Nature is a great healer," he maintained. "That leg is stronger today than ever before."

I was the plaintiff's attorney, and I said to the doctor, "Well, we all want strong legs. Perhaps we should go to you, Doctor, and pay you to break our legs so you can operate on them and make them better than ever."

He lost the case on its merits, but his absurd statements on the stand didn't help him any.

The cross-examination

This is a crisis point. Your friendly lawyer is gone, and in his place is an attorney who is only too ready and willing to tear down your testimony.

Don't panic. The plaintiff's lawyer has a tougher job than you—*if* you've prepared your defense properly. He has to invade *your* area of expertise—medicine—and prove his contentions that you went wrong.

However, never underestimate the medical knowledge of a good plaintiff's lawyer. In every case he tries, he takes a crash course on the clinical problems involved. He may even know more about a particular problem than you do. Treat him with respect. If you don't, he might turn the tables on you.

I remember in one case I tried, the doctor came off the stand in a surly mood after cross-examination.

"Mr. Belli," he growled, "let me congratulate you on a very superficial knowledge of medicine."

I bowed and replied, "Doctor, I would like to go at least as far as you. But honesty does not permit it."

So when the cross-examiner takes over, regard him respectfully, consider his questions carefully, and answer calmly. Don't respond too quickly. Give your attorney time to object if a question is wrongly put.

Don't be misled by the cross-examiner who's polite and ingratiating—even sympathetic. He may be the toughest cross-examiner of all.

Whether the cross-examiner comes on soft or strong, beware of the following types of questions:

• "Have you rehearsed your testimony?" The implication is that you and your lawyer have made up a lot of false or misleading responses.

The proper reply: "I have discussed the case at length with my attorney, and he has explained to me the legal points that are involved."

A note a warning: Don't memorize parts of your testimony for delivery on the stand. A good plaintiff's lawyer will spot those set little speeches, and he'll move quickly to break them up with distracting questions. The witness loses track of what he's memorized and is sometimes literally left speechless. Just get your facts firmly set in your mind, and your responses will flow easily and effectively from those facts.

• "I believe you spent 30 minutes in the operating room, and your fee was $3,000." Translation: You're not only a butcher—you're a money-mad butcher.

Correct response: "I spent (whatever the precise time was) in the operating room, and my fee included extensive pre-op workup and post-op care."

• "Are you board-certified?" The intention here is to undermine your credentials. If you're not board-certified, say so—the cross-examiner will know the truth, and if you deviate from it, he'll nail you as a liar.

You might say, "I'm board-eligible. I haven't taken the test because I don't feel it's necessary for my practice."

- "It's a fact that such-and-such is the case, so my question to you is—" The purpose here is to slip in a misstatement or exaggeration. Respond by saying, "I don't accept that as a fact. My impression is that this is the fact—" and then explain your interpretation.

- "Do all doctors agree with your medical opinion?" The cross-examiner is hoping you'll say Yes so he can clobber you with authoritative opinions in opposition.

Beat him to the punch and say, "Many medical issues allow for honest differences of opinion. There are doctors who might disagree with me, but based on my training and experience, I believe my opinion is correct in this particular instance."

No matter what the question is, don't take on the cross-examiner in a verbal joust. In olden times, when legal action was literally trial by combat, lawyers were swordsmen or pugilists. Today's attorneys are skilled with words rather than swords, at punch lines rather than punches.

Unless you're absolutely sure of yourself, and willing to risk looking silly on the witness stand, don't cross words with a cross-examiner. Consider the following examples of doctors who left themselves open to put-downs:

- One doctor I was cross-examining seemed overly impelled to defend his integrity.

"Don't you think I'm telling the truth?" he hotly blurted.

"There's no doubt about that in my mind, Doctor," I responded, "but there seems to be some question in yours."

- A riled cardiologist snapped at his cross-examiner, "Counselor, the trouble with you is that you're not like me. You don't have a heart!"

The attorney replied, "Doctor, the plaintiff in this case also had a heart. I intend to prove to this jury that he is dead today, and his wife is widowed, because you overlooked the fact that there was a clot in an artery of that heart."

- The doctor on the stand kept smiling—even chuckling at times—at the cross-examiner's questions, implying that they were jokes.

The attorney finally said, "Doctor, you seem to think this case is a laughing matter. If so, please explain why that is to the jury."

That wiped the smile off the doctor's face.

Ordinarily, the courtroom is no place for mirth, although humor is permissible at times. John J. Bower, a New York malpractice defense attorney, fondly remembers an elderly surgeon who was so at ease during his cross-examination that when asked if an appendix has a function, he replied, "Oh, yes, certainly."

Taken off stride by this unorthodox view, the attorney asked, "What is it?"

"It keeps surgeons eating," the venerable doctor replied, and the judge and jury joined him in a good laugh.

Don't try that yourself unless you have a quick wit and a very appealing personality.

Probably the greatest fear a doctor on the stand has is that he will fall victim to a lawyer's dirty tricks. I don't deny that this used to be a stock in trade of some cross-examiners. Just one example:

The doctor-defendant was doing very well under cross-examination. He answered questions calmly and confidently, and the opposition lawyer just couldn't shake his testimony. Finally the lawyer returned to the plaintiff's table for a brief conference with an assistant. The cross-examination resumed.

Shortly afterward—in violation of the usual rules of courtroom conduct—the bailiff passed an unsigned note up to the doctor on the stand.

Suddenly, the doctor's face turned crimson. He scrunched down in his seat and began contorting his body, hardly mindful of the tough questions the plaintiff's lawyer was putting to him. It looked as if the doctor was having trouble with the truth. In fact, he was troubled by the contents of the note, which read, "Doctor, your fly is open."

His fly wasn't open. The note was a concoction of the plaintiff's lawyer and his assistant.

That happened many years ago. Today such shenanigans would bring down the wrath of the judge on an offending lawyer. In other words, dirty tricks of that type are largely a thing of the past. Don't worry about them.

What you should worry about is the lawyer who tries to provoke you to anger. One instance:

The weary defendant had been kept on the stand for more than an hour by an attorney who bombarded him continually with exasperating questions, many of which cast doubt on his integrity. With mounting rage, the doctor began shouting his responses, sometimes shaking his fist.

Finally he reached the breaking point. When the lawyer handed him a heavy volume of hospital records and asked him to turn to a certain page, the doctor threw the whole thing at the lawyer, knocking his glasses to the floor and cutting his forehead. The jury stared in horror as the lawyer just stood there, blood trickling down his face.

In short, your worst enemy in the courtroom is anger. A doctor is supposed to be a person in control. When you lose control, you lose credibility.

If an attorney comes roaring at you, don't roar back. That's what he wants you to do, thus diminishing your professional stature.

Keep your composure. Remember the basic principle of Oriental martial arts—defeat an enemy through the force of his own assault. In the face of the lawyer's heated questions, remain cool. Don't flinch from his bombast. Just respond to it politely.

The contrast between the two of you will soon be obvious to the jurors, and they'll instinctively side with you. Nobody likes a bully.

A machine-gun barrage of questions is another tactic of an aggressive cross-examiner. Slow him down by taking your time in answering. Occasionally say, "I'm sorry, but I don't understand that last question," and get him to repeat it. That will spike his gun, or at least decrease the rate of fire.

Don't volunteer anything. Answer the cross-examiner's questions as briefly as possible, preferably with a Yes or No. If you go beyond that, you may provide more ammunition and open up a whole new field of warfare. Your main objective is to get off the stand and out of the war zone as soon as you can, and with your defense intact.

The exit

When you leave the stand, don't give vent to your feelings. Some witnesses, figuring they've won, will grin at the spectators or wave to friends. One doctor even clasped his hands over his head like a triumphant prizefighter.

Don't anticipate victory. The only thing certain in a lawsuit is the expense.

On the other hand, don't tag yourself as a loser. Don't sigh deeply, mop your brow, look dejected, hang your head, or slink out of the courtroom.

Remember, the judge and jury are still observing you. Leave the stand in a composed manner, and unless you've been instructed to remain in the courtroom, walk out with dignity.

Whether you win or lose, you may want to countersue the plaintiff. Can you? Is it worth doing, and how do you do it? Find out in the following chapter.

32

*W*hat about a countersuit?

This legal route is open to you under certain circumstances, but it's a tough road to travel.

━━━

When a malpractice complaint is dumped on a doctor's desk, his first reaction is usually shock. Then comes anger, and a burning desire to "get even." That's only natural. When you're hit, you want to hit back.

Pulling off a successful countersuit may even seem easy. California orthopedic surgeon Donald R. Huene did it in spectacular style. After being sued for malpractice, he discovered the lawyer had filed the case without the patient's consent. The case was eventually dropped, and Huene countersued the lawyer for malicious prosecution.

"I not only thought the suit was meritless," explains Huene, "but I felt an important principle was involved. If a doctor performs a procedure on a patient without informed consent, he can be held liable. I felt the same principle should apply to a lawyer."

Unable to find a satisfactory attorney, Huene filed the

countersuit himself and argued it through a trial court and the appeals process all the way to the state supreme court.

That took five years, during which, Huene admits, he became "obsessed" with the suit and spent much of his spare time on it. On the other hand, because he acted as his own attorney, his legal expenses came to only $700.

It all paid off when the supreme court returned a verdict agreeing with Huene's main contention: "An attorney has no more right to sue a person without the consent of the client than does a physician to undertake a particular surgical procedure without the consent of the patient." Huene was awarded damages of $45,000.

Obviously this is a highly unusual case. Few doctors have Huene's knack for the law, nor his skill and tenacity in fighting a difficult case right down to the end.

So what's a more realistic view of countersuits? Are they worthwhile or a waste of time?

To answer those general questions, we turn to the specifics of what it takes to win a countersuit.

Are you on solid legal ground?

Some doctors are so incensed when a patient sues that they want to file an immediate countersuit. That can't be done. To win a countersuit, a physician must first obtain a "favorable termination" of the malpractice suit. This can be achieved if the plaintiff drops the suit, if the case is dismissed by pretrial motion, or if a trial court returns a verdict in the doctor's favor.

Even if a case is dropped, there can be complications. A New York doctor, for example, filed a countersuit after a malpractice suit was discontinued. The countersuit was knocked down by a judge who ruled that the malpractice suit had been discontinued by agreement of both parties. The plaintiff, the judge held, must drop the suit of his own volition.

What if a suit is settled without a trial? Can the doctor-defendant then proceed with a countersuit? Not usually. In most settlements, each side provides the other with a release of all claims. That doesn't constitute a favorable termination for the doctor.

However, let's say a physician emerges from the malpractice case a clear winner and files a countersuit. To again come out a winner, he must prove the following three points:

1. The suit was brought without probable cause.

This means that the doctor must show (1) that no reasonable attorney would have filed the case, or (2) that the attorney's investigation of the case was grossly insufficient, assuming that proper investigation would have cleared the doctor at the outset. For example:

Kentucky radiologist George F. Drasin was accused in a malpractice complaint of "performing in a careless and negligent manner," thereby breaking the shoulder of a patient in a hospital emergency room. The patient, a 65-year-old man, had been brought to the ER after suffering a massive coronary occlusion. The breaking of the shoulder was alleged to have occurred during defibrillation.

Drasin protested that as a diagnostic radiologist, he'd had no direct contact with the patient. He'd simply read X-rays that had *already* been taken of a fracture in the shoulder. Yet he was included along with a number of other doctors in a "gang-suit" action.

Three months later, Drasin was dropped from the case. However, he says, "The knowledge that I'd been slapped with a [$500,000] lawsuit on such flimsy grounds made me downright angry. Worse, I found I'd lost a lot of joy in my work. I was painfully aware that any of my patients—most of whom I never even met—might take it into their heads to sue me for a bad result that I had nothing to do with."

Moreover, Drasin's referrals had slumped more than 20 percent in the months following the malpractice suit.

Drasin then joined in a countersuit with another doctor who'd been dismissed from the malpractice action. The countersuit, seeking $95,000, was directed against the two lawyers who had initiated the malpractice case, accusing them of malicious prosecution.

This in effect was a test case—the first medical-malpractice countersuit in Kentucky. Under the law of that state, malice is interpreted as "wrongful purpose." It can be inferred if a lawyer brings a suit without "probable cause"—"which certainly described what [the lawyer] had done to us," says Drasin.

The jury agreed, awarding Drasin and the other doctor $10,000 each in compensatory damages, and $15,000 in punitive damages. However, the case was appealed to the state supreme court, which upheld the awards but ruled that only one lawyer could be held liable.

2. The plaintiff or his attorney acted with malice.

Malice, of course, is a deliberate attempt to cause damage, suffering, or harm to another. In some cases, that's relatively easy to prove. A female family physician in California, for example, was driven out of private practice by malicious gossip spread by a former patient during a malpractice suit. In a countersuit, the jury deliberated only a short while before awarding the FP $100,000 against the former patient and her attorney.

More often than not, though, malice is a tricky issue to decide. Generally, it means more than simple spite. Evidence must be produced to show that a malpractice suit was filed and prosecuted with reckless abandon, and with little or no regard for the doctor's reputation.

A few instances where reckless abandon has been proved in countersuits: the doctor is sued with the intent of forcing him into a quick settlement; the plaintiff's lawyer hasn't consulted any medical experts about the validity of a malpractice charge; a malpractice suit has been filed with an ulterior motive, such as to compel the doctor to give evidence in a deposition against others in the case; the plaintiff's lawyer failed to sufficiently investigate the medical records before filing a malpractice suit; the plaintiff's charges are based only on speculation, rather than facts.

Opinions differ from state to state on what constitutes reckless abandon. In Indiana, an appeals court held that "mere negligence in asserting a [medical malpractice] claim is not sufficient to subject an attorney to liability." It added that an attorney has probable cause to sue if he believes "the claim merits litigation against the defendant...on the basis of the facts known to the attorney when the suit was commenced."

An opposite conclusion was reached by the Kansas Supreme Court, which stated that an attorney cannot act on the assumption that his client's version of the case is correct. The court declared that the plaintiff's attorney should also get the doctor's side of the story.

In short, before you get into a countersuit, make sure you know what the law holds in your state regarding malice and reckless abandon.

3. The doctor suffered damages from the suit.

It used to be that you had to prove dollar damages such as a significant loss of income or a sharp drop in patient load. Most states now have a wider interpretation of damages, including loss of reputation, general emotional distress, related health problems, and the cost of defending the malpractice suit. Some juries are also awarding punitive damages along with actual damages.

Even if you know you can clear those three legal hurdles— probable cause, malice, and damages—it may not be advisable to proceed with a countersuit unless you can satisfactorily answer these questions:

Can you bear up under the financial burden?

Let's go back to the case of Dr. Huene, who won a countersuit award of $45,000. That makes him sound like a financial winner. Actually, if he hadn't been able to act as his own attorney, he might well have come out a financial loser. Legal fees in that complex case could easily have exceeded the amount of the award.

Even in a routine countersuit, one going through a trial court, legal costs can add up to $30,000 and more, all of which must come out of the doctor's pocket. If a case has to go through the whole appeals process, many thousands of dollars more will be needed—and that will all be gone if the verdict goes against the doctor. You also have to figure in money lost through disruptions in the doctor's practice.

Don't think you can easily find a lawyer who's willing to take a countersuit on a contingency basis. The outcome is too dicey. Even if a case is won, the award is usually low, sometimes only a few thousand dollars. The top award so far in the whole country is $175,000.

Why these low figures? There are four answers: (1) Juries generally feel doctors don't really need the money. (2) Most plaintiffs don't have the resources to pay big awards. (3) Even if a plaintiff's lawyer has done wrong, the damage doesn't compare with medical malpractice cases where patients are left crippled, brain-damaged, or dead. (4) And although an award may be won in a trial court, it's often taken back on the appellate court level. Countersuit victories for doctors have been upheld on appeal in only a few states.

Some countersuit assistance is provided to doctors by state medical societies, especially in California, Florida, Georgia, Indiana, Michigan, and New York. This mostly consists of technical and legal guidance, but financial aid is available in some instances.

If vindication on principle is more important to you than economic revenge, there's an alternative to the high cost of a countersuit. In several states, doctors who have prevailed in malpractice suits have requested and obtained letters of apology from plaintiffs and lawyers. Those letters have then been published in local newspapers or medical journals, helping to erase any smudges the doctors might feel remained on their reputations.

Can you cope with the emotional demands placed on you by a countersuit?

Many doctors file countersuits without realizing that they in effect will be reliving the bitter experiences of the malpractice suits against them. Beware: The wheels of justice grind ever so slowly, and in time that grinding takes its toll on defendants and plaintiffs alike.

It requires two to five years for a doctor to win a malpractice suit. A countersuit will last another two to five years. That means a doctor will have to go through two arduous trials and spend from four to 10 years fighting on the legal front. It's tough going, not only for the doctor but his family as well.

Some doctors find it's not worth it. Of 27 countersuit cases selected by the California Medical Association for financial and other support, about one-third were not pursued because the physicians changed their minds about getting back into the legal fray, with all its worry, pain, and drain. The principal reasons: strains in family relationships, and deterioration of the doctor's practice.

Some doctors back off from a countersuit when they see it could boomerang on them. A defendant-attorney or plaintiff who wins a countersuit can then counter-countersue the doctor. It hasn't happened yet, but it definitely could.

Let me emphasize that I'm not saying a doctor *shouldn't* countersue a patient or lawyer who has unfairly or frivolously brought a malpractice suit. I'm simply pointing out what's needed to win a countersuit. It's not enough just to be angry— you must have a strong case, and a strong constitution to travel a long, hard road.

Looking beyond that road to the future, what malpractice hazards loom ahead for doctors? We'll wrap that all up in the next and concluding chapter.

33

The malpractice risks you'll face in the future

Here's how to avoid future shock from medico-legal trends now in the formative stage.

The law evolves and changes as our lives take on new patterns. Only a relatively few years ago, the alphabet soup made up of PPO, DRG, and DNR wasn't on a doctor's daily menu. Now it is, and many doctors are tentatively tasting it, wondering whether it's going to be good or bad for them.

In the case of the Preferred Provider Organizations and Diagnosis-Related Groups, the principal concern of the medical profession right now is economic. Will these new developments prove a boon or a bane to a doctor's income? In Do Not Resuscitate orders, the dilemma is largely ethical. In issuing such orders, is a doctor doing what's professionally right?

Hidden in the alphabet soup is another ingredient—the law. What new liabilities are developing for physicians? How can doctors cope with them?

Let's consider those questions first, then move on to other
trends that are reshaping the medical malpractice picture.
Physicians who take note of what's happening now will be better able to defend themselves in the future.

Preferred Provider Organizations

PPOs appeal mostly to doctors who are seeking larger patient
loads. By contract, the doctor agrees to discount his fees and
submit to rigorous utilization review. In return, the PPO
promises to funnel new patients to him.

Fine. But what happens if the contract is terminated? In a
legal sense, plenty happens—although that's often ignored in
the contracts.

Not long ago, for example, a doctor in Southern California
ended his PPO contract on a Friday. The next week, a PPO
patient came in who'd been under treatment. The doctor said
that he was sorry but he couldn't treat the patient any longer
unless he paid privately.

Angered, the patient consulted a lawyer, who contacted the
doctor and pointed out, quite rightly, that he'd abandoned the
patient. Rather than get into a legal hassle, the doctor then
continued to treat the patient without compensation.

Moral: Before you sign a PPO contract, make sure there's
provision in there to deal with the legal aspects of ending the
agreement.

Another liability arises under the referral limitations of a
PPO contract. Usually, a referral can be made only to another
PPO doctor if the patient is to get a discount. If that doctor
turns out to be incompetent and a malpractice suit results, the
referring physician might also be named as a defendant.

Will it do any good to protest that you *had* to send the patient to another PPO doctor under the demands of your contract? No. By law, you can't allow contractual restrictions to
alter the proper standard of care.

Moral: Find out in advance the names and locations of all
referral doctors, and make sure they're fully qualified.

Physicians going into PPO contracts today face another legal pitfall. They figure that if they get into a malpractice situation with a PPO patient, their own carrier will cover them. Maybe not. Most policies, as they're written currently, deny or limit coverage for liability assumed under a contract.

That's not all. In a recent survey by the California Medical Association, only about a quarter of the PPOs in the state were found to carry their own liability insurance. In short, a doctor could wind up paying for a PPO's negligence.

Moral: Unless you're willing to go bare for PPO patients, don't sign unless you're sure you're sufficiently covered for malpractice.

Diagnosis-Related Groups

You hear a lot about how this form of prospective payment for Medicare is going to hold down hospital costs. You hear little or nothing about how the DRG system can entangle you in a malpractice suit.

Let's start with liability for undertreatment. A patient is in the hospital for a certain ailment that, under the DRG system, is allowed a certain number of days for treatment. When the allotted time is up, the patient is ousted.

What if the disease then worsens? Can the patient sue for malpractice? If so, who is sued?

Although there's no specific case law on this yet under the DRG system, I can see serious implications ahead for doctors and hospitals. One harbinger is a 1982 case. A patient sued the state because she lost a leg after a Medi-Cal [Medicaid] utilization nurse and a physician-consultant for the agency cut short her hospital stay. A jury awarded her $500,000.

A significant point: The patient did not sue her physicians, because they protested her removal from the hospital. So remember that if you're ever in a similar situation under the DRG system. If, in your best medical judgment, the patient should not be removed, make your feelings known to hospital authorities and record your position in the hospital chart.

That will afford you at least some malpractice protection. Physicians who unquestionably give in to pressure to release patients will come under the legal gun along with the hospital.

Bad faith can also come into play. A doctor has a duty to provide not only care consistent with community standards, but all the care that's medically necessary.

Therefore, if a patient is released from the hospital while still in medical need, the doctor might well be charged with failing in a fundamental duty. If it can be proved that any treatment was withheld because of financial considerations— that is, holding down hospital costs—the doctor can also be accused of conflict of interest. That constitutes bad faith, which can result in costly punitive damages that aren't usually covered by professional liability insurance.

In sum, cost-containment in health care is important, but it must not jeopardize the quality of care. Place your patients' interests first, well before any financial considerations.

Do Not Resuscitate orders

Many doctors now shy away from writing such an order on a patient's chart. Everybody remembers the two California physicians who were accused of murder after they removed life-support systems from a terminally comatose patient.

An appellate court finally exonerated those two doctors, but not before they'd been put through a legal wringer. The judge ruled: A physician who makes a reasonable medical decision cannot be prosecuted.

The doctors' decision in that case was clearly reasonable—it was backed by the signatures of half-a-dozen next of kin and the testimony of an authoritative medical ethicist.

However, if a DNR order is issued without proper discussion with the patient's family, or if a coded DNR sticker is arbitrarily attached to a chart, trouble may well be in store for the doctors involved.

The main difficulty is that no really good guidelines have been laid down for doctors to follow when a patient is hopelessly ill, but still clings technically to life. Some day, those guidelines will be in place, but until then, DNR orders will be an increasingly tough problem for doctors to handle.

Meanwhile, to safeguard yourself, discuss the problem with the patient—if possible—and the family. Be sure that they understand what's involved. Don't pressure them into making a decision. If there's any disagreement in the family, give them time to reach accord.

Consult with other doctors in the hospital, particularly those who are knowledgeable about this problem. If necessary, call in outside experts. Bring family members into these meetings and invite them to contribute to the consultation.

Make sure the hospital staff knows what you're doing and why you're doing it. In the case of the two California doctors, a nurse didn't understand why all life-support systems were withdrawn. The murder charge stemmed from her call to the district attorney's office.

Include all pertinent details in your chart notes. And don't abbreviate anything.

Don't rely on oral DNR orders, coded stickers on the patient's chart, or red circles on a list of room numbers where terminally ill patients are located. These maneuvers may be interpreted as efforts to hide something. They might also lead to a wrong patient being deprived of life-support systems.

Greater emphasis on keeping up

A GP had been practicing in a small city for almost 40 years. After examining a middle-aged housewife and running some tests, he told her, "You're going to need a mastectomy."

She hesitated, then said, "I'm scared of operations."

"You needn't be," the doctor replied. "A lot of women have this operation."

But this woman didn't—nor did she seek other medical advice. She died, and her husband and children sued.

On the stand, the GP made a favorable impression—until the plaintiff's attorney began questioning him about breast-cancer treatment. The doctor admitted he knew very little about lumpectomy with primary radiation therapy, an alternative treatment that the patient probably would have accepted and that might have saved her life.

The plaintiff's attorney later told me: "The doctor was well liked in the community, and the jury really wanted to help him. But they just couldn't when they found out he was not familiar with all the current options for treatment. They gave the family a large award."

That kind of scenario is bound to occur again and again. With all the rapid changes in medical knowledge and technology, judges and juries will become more and more interested in how well doctors are keeping up.

The doctor who isn't up to date in medicine will probably be out of luck in court.

A closer look at consultations and referrals

When a young boy developed some strange bruises on the inside of his legs and began to limp, his parents took him to an orthopedist. After examining the boy, the orthopedist decided that he had simply bruised his legs in a fall.

"Just keep an eye on him," he instructed the parents. "If he doesn't improve, bring him back."

The parents returned with the boy a week later. The doctor did another examination and repeated his instruction to watch the condition closely.

Ultimately, the boy's legs had to be amputated because of purpura fulminans. If he'd been referred promptly to a pediatrician, his legs probably could have been saved. The parents sued the orthopedist on grounds that he had failed to make a referral, and they won a large award.

The point here is that generalists aren't the only doctors who have a duty to bring specialists into complicated cases. Courts today are taking the view that specialists themselves should call for help when they get in over their heads.

I talk to a lot of doctors who end up in situations like the orthopedist's, and I ask them, "Why didn't you refer the patient, or seek a consultation?"

The answers fall into three categories: (1) "I felt that I could handle the case myself." (2) "I was trying to hold down the patient's costs." (3) "He was a regular patient, and I didn't want to lose him. The competition is rough these days."

So basically, what we're dealing with are economics and ego. The courts won't allow either of them to be placed above good patient care.

More and better expert witnesses

I often speak at medical meetings. During one recent assembly of 600 physicians, I asked how many would be willing to testify against the defendant in a meritorious malpractice case. More than half the doctors in the auditorium raised their hands.

We've come a long way from the days of the "conspiracy of silence," when doctors refused to testify against each other, even in the most horrendous of cases. And I see the trend continuing, with more and more topflight specialists making themselves available as expert witnesses.

Recently, for example, I described a case to one of the most prestigious neurosurgeons in the world and asked if he would testify as an expert witness at the trial. Although he had never appeared professionally in a court before, he agreed, saying he thought he could contribute something important.

I've also noticed an increasing number of agencies that offer to provide lawyers with expert medical witnesses. Now, some of these doctors are simply out for the money—whores, if you like—but there are also many competent ones. And plaintiffs' attorneys soon learn who they are and use them.

The result is that more and more highly qualified expert medical witnesses are testifying against defendants in malpractice cases. Physicians can no longer feel they're going against someone they can easily show up.

They can also expect to go up against more expert witnesses

who are non-MDs, such as chiropractors, podiatrists, and
nurses. Yes, nurses. In a recent appellate court test in Texas,
an LVN was allowed to testify as an expert witness in a malpractice case involving a 15-year-old girl who had suffered
permanent brain damage as an ICU patient.

I personally have used chiropractors in a number of cases,
and they're very effective. The key is to keep the testimony of
non-MDs strictly within their own fields. Often they make
more sense to jurors than the MD defendants.

I'm not trying to build up the scientific credentials of chiropractors and other non-MDs. They have their failings, and
some of them are outright frauds, but the good ones are developing a considerable following. Some of those followers end
up on juries.

A sharper breed of plaintiff's attorney

The number of lawyers who specialize in medico-legal matters
is increasing dramatically. Some are even beginning to sub-
specialize. One in my firm recently announced his intention to
concentrate solely on birth-injury cases.

There'll be more of such subspecialization in the future.
Some attorneys even favor a series of special bar exams that
would enable them to qualify for licensure in the various sub-
specialties. Consequently, more defendant-physicians will
face attorneys who are highly knowledgeable in very specific
areas of medicine.

Doctors' countersuits against lawyers are also helping to
produce a better breed of malpractice attorney. The incompetents are being weeded out.

Contingency fees play a part here, too, because attorneys
who take a malpractice case on that basis have to become expert in the medical details of a case to ensure a good chance of
winning. If they don't win, of course, they get nothing back—
not even the money they've put into the case.

And legal firms are investing big money—$250,000 and
more in some of my own cases that have gone to trial. When

that kind of money is on the line, you can bet only the most skilled attorneys will be at work for the plaintiff.

More electronic magic

Not long ago, I took on a case in which my staff and I had to wade through hundreds of medical papers and books to pinpoint possible causes of rare affliction. The research involved months of time, much effort, and considerable expense. Today, by computer, we can do a far better job of research in a fraction of the time, with a minimum of expense and effort.

And there's more ahead. A New York research company is setting up a computerized data-retrieval system that can provide lawyers with all the standard case law needed to conduct a suit *and* tell a plaintiff's attorney his chances of winning—based on the data available, the disposition of the courts in his area, and the recent history of the defendants. The company will also research the history of a medical expert scheduled to testify.

In short, computers are now a valuable aid to attorneys—defense as well as plaintiff's—and these mechanical marvels will be doing even more in the future.

Videotape is also coming on strong. Plaintiff's attorneys are using it more and more often in depositions, thus capturing a doctor's demeanor and technique as well as his words. In one instance, I spotted a doctor holding a surgical instrument wrongly while demonstrating how to do a certain procedure.

Some doctors even consider appearing on tape a fun thing to do, like a home movie. Don't fall into that trap. A taped deposition is as serious as an appearance in court, and it's essential that it be treated as such.

Taping has other uses for a plaintiff's attorney. In one case, an expert witness died before the trial, but the attorney still had his testimony on videotape. It helped convince the jury that the defendant-doctor had been negligent. In another case that demonstrates the dramatic possibilities of courtroom electronics, the jurors listened to testimony recorded by the patient before her death. They ultimately awarded her family more than $3 million.

More "shotgun" cases

There'll be an increasing number of multiple-defendant malpractice complaints as doctors increasingly work in teams on cases. There are two basic reasons for this "sue everybody" approach.

1. Although an injury may be apparent, it may also be difficult to pinpoint exactly who's to blame.

2. Too often with the team approach, there's a lack of effective communication, and slip-ups occur. Just one example:

A young woman went to a family physician, complaining of pain in one leg. The FP diagnosed a femoral fracture and referred the patient to an orthopedist, who then repaired the break.

While the woman was still in the hospital, a test indicated phlebitis. So an internist and a hematologist entered the case. An anticoagulant was prescribed, and the patient remained on the medication long after her discharge. She eventually bled to death.

Not one of those doctors had tested the patient's blood. All apparently assumed that one of the others had done it, but no one had bothered to ask.

Because of this breakdown in vital communication, and because no doctor could be singled out for total blame, all had to be named in a suit brought by the widower. All eventually contributed to a very large settlement.

There'll be more situations like this unless doctors go back to what they routinely used to do—get together and discuss treatment, then check with each other regularly on what they're doing. Appointing a team coordinator would also help.

More suits for birth injuries

Some specialties and procedures have long been recognized as particularly risky. The danger area that is in the medico-legal limelight right now, and will become increasingly so in the future, is prenatal care and delivery. Doctors involved in such cases are being sued for malpractice at a greater rate than ever before, and awards have soared well into the millions, especially for infants who are brain-damaged, or born with drug-related defects.

In one recent case, a senior obstetrician at a hospital noted fetal heartbeat irregularities when the mother was admitted in labor. Though he left orders to be called as soon as any irregularities recurred, he wasn't notified until more than seven hours after the recurrence. By that time, the operating room was unavailable, the Caesarean section was delayed an hour and a half, and the baby was born with brain damage.

The resulting malpractice suit was settled out of court for payments that will total millions over the child's lifetime.

In another case, a court ruled that the mother had the right to sue not only for malpractice, but also for the emotional distress she suffered when her child was still-born.

As for drug-related birth defects, I know of one Los Angeles attorney who's currently handling at least 30 cases involving limb-deformed children.

The trend is obvious: Any doctor who does obstetrics will be held to the highest possible standards, from diagnosis of pregnancy through the delivery.

The same goes for care provided immediately after birth. In fact, the St. Paul insurance companies report that improper treatment of birth-related problems is the most common malpractice claim filed against pediatricians who don't do surgery.

Do all these growing risks mean that doctors are headed for catastrophe?

Not at all. Medicine is and always will be a needed and a revered profession, and physicians will continue to command respect for their devotion, responsibility, skills, and intelligence. The vast majority of them are capable of not only surmounting the risks that I've mentioned, but of emerging as better practitioners.

The end result can only be something that we all want— better patient care.

*I*ndex

Abandonment
  emergency room referrals
    and, 108
  liability and, 24-25
  Preferred Provider
    Organizations and, 202
  See also Withdrawal of
    treatment
Alcohol abuse
  diagnosis and, 79
  medical records and, 93
Allergies
  documentation and, 87
  medications and, 83-85
Alternative treatment
  informed consent, 99-100
  See also Consultation;
    Second opinions
American Medical
  Association (AMA)
  diagnosis and, 76
  freedom of choice and, 23
  incompetency and, 1
  medication side effects and,
    85
Anger, 191
Apologies, 198
Appeals
  costs of, 33
  countersuits and, 198
Attorney (physician's)
  judges and, 169, 170

  selection of, 135-138
  trial preparation and, 145-
    149
Attorney (plaintiff's)
  blaming of, 1
  communication with, 146-
    147
  competency of, 2, 208-209
  countersuits and, 193-194,
    195-196
  ethics of, 21
  information about, 148
  judges and, 169-170
Availability (of physician), 13-
  14

Beatus, Morris, 125-126
Billing, 119-122
  excessive, 121-122
  fraud and, 120-121
  implied consent and, 120
  sensitivity in, 4, 119-120
Birth injuries, 210-211
  See also Pediatrics
Borrowed-servant rule, 71-72
Bower, John J., 190

Callousness
  depositions and, 140
  malpractice suits and, 14-15
  medication prescription
    and, 82

laboratory test reporting
and, 16-17
See also Indifference;
Insensitivity
Chiropractors, 208
Claims made insurance, 28
Codefendants, 147
Colleagues
communications with, 147
criticism by, 8-9
insurance coverage and, 33-
34
liability and, 55-59
medical records and, 93-94
medication and, 83
Communication
attorneys and, 137
codefendants and, 147
colleagues and, 57-58, 147
emergencies and, 7
indifference and, 13, 14
misunderstandings and, 6-7
plaintiffs, 147
plaintiffs' attorney, 146-147
plaintiffs' family, 43-44
procedure explanations,
44-45
"shotgun" cases, 210
test results reporting, 16-17
Competency
attorneys and, 137-138
See also Incompetence
Complainers (patient type),
36-37
Compliance. *See* Patient
compliance; Refusal of
treatment
Confidentiality
employees and, 53-54
medical records, 90-91
Conflict of interest, 136
Consent. *See* Informed
consent; Implied consent
Conspiracy of silence, 8-9,
207
Consultation
diagnosis and, 78-80

Do Not Resuscitate orders
and, 205
importance of, 206-207
See also Alternative
treatment; Second
opinions
Consumerist-type patients,
37, 45
Continuing medical
education, 205-206
Contributory negligence,
151-155
Control, events beyond
physician's, 5-6
Costs. *See* Legal costs
Countersuits, 193-199
colleagues and, 59
damages requirement and,
197
emotional demands of, 199
financial burden of, 197-198
legal grounds for, 194-195
malice requirement and,
196-197
plaintiff's lawyer and, 21
risk of, 2
settlements and, 137
without probable cause
requirement and, 195-196
Coverups, 93-94
Cross-examination, 187-92
Cynics (patient type), 38

Defense
contributory negligence,
151-155
expert witnesses, 157-162
judges and, 169-172
Defense Research Institute,
166
Delegation, 52-53
Demonstrative evidence,
179-182
Deposition, 139-144
expert witnesses and, 161-
162
guardedness in, 141-142

importance of, 139-141
intimidation and, 142
leading questions in, 143
timing in, 143-144
videotaped, 209
Detectives. *See* Private
  investigators;
  Investigation
Diagnosis, 75-80
consultation and, 79-80
inexact science
  consideration, 75-76
laboratory tests and,
  76-77
throughness in, 77-79
See also Laboratory tests
Diagnosis-Related Groups
  (DRGs), 203-204
Direct examination, 185-187
Doctor-shoppers. *See*
  Consumerist-type patients
Documentation
contributory negligence
  and, 153-154
emergency rooms and, 109
hospital nurses and, 71
medical advice and, 5
medication and, 87
patient compliance and, 37-
  38
telephone treatment and,
  117
withdrawal of treatment
  and, 25
See also Medical records
Do Not Resuscitate orders,
  204-205
Dosage (medication), 86
Drasin, George F., 195-196
Drugs. *See* Medication
Duty to cooperate, 29

Emergencies
decisions in, 7
treatment refusal and, 23-
  24
Emergency rooms, 107-111

admissions procedures,
  108-109
attending physician
  differences with, 110-111
communication problems
  and, 110
documentation and, 109
transfers and, 111
See also Hospitals
Emotional costs, 19-22
Employees, 47-54
confidentiality and, 53-54
delegation and, 52-53
informed consent and, 95-
  96
liability and, 47
malpractice suits and, 4
medical practice by, 50-52
reception and, 48-49
supervisory tips for,
  49-50
See also Nurses
Entrapment, 131, 132-133
Evidence
countersuits and, 196
demonstrative evidence,
  179-182
medical records and, 186
See also Documentation;
  Medical records
Expertise, practicing beyond,
  15-16
Expert witnesses, 157-162,
  163-168
colleagues and, 8-9
discrediting of, 164-167
improvements in, 207-208
investigation of, 163-164
reforms and, 167-168
selection of, 159-162
testimony of, 157-159
Explanation. *See* Procedure
  explanation
Extraordinary circumstances,
  7
See also Emergencies;
  Emergency rooms

Face-to-face communication,
14
See also Communication
Fager, Donald, 167-168
Family (patient's), 41-46
   communication with, 43-44
   diagnosis and, 78
   Do Not Resuscitate orders
      and, 204, 205
   explanation of procedures
      and, 44-45
   informed consent and, 97
   liability and, 41-42
Family (physician's), 185
Fees. *See* Billing
First-aid treatment, 24
Flatterer (patient type), 35-36
Fraud, 120-121
Full disclosure requirement,
   30
Future trends, 201-211

Gilchrist, Edgar, 162
Glickman, David R., 105, 106
Good Samaritan situations, 24
Grievers (patient type), 38-39
Griffith, James, 130
Group practice
   insurance coverage and, 28
   liability and, 56-57
   See also Partnerships; Solo
      practice
Guarantees
   employees and, 51
   implied, 17
   misunderstandings and, 4
   warning signs and, 37
Guarriello, Donna Lee, 72
Guilt, 45

Handwriting, 86-87
Hasty, Frederick E., III, 34
Hayes, John D., 182
Health insurance carriers
   second opinions and, 103,
      104

See also Malpractice
   insurance
Honesty, 186-187
Horsley, Jack E., 9, 152
Hospitals
   conditions in, 68-70
   Diagnostic-Related Groups
      (DRGs) and, 230-204
   divide-and-conquer tactics,
      73-74
   emergency rooms, 107-111
   investigations of, 126-127
   lawyer assignments and,
      136
   liability and, 61-74
   nursing staff in, 70-73
   policies of, 62-68
   telephone treatment and,
      117
   See also Emergency rooms
Huene, Donald R., 193, 197
Humor
   cynicism and, 38
   insensitivity in, 11-12
   testimony and, 189-190

Ignoring the patient. *See*
   Callousness; Indifference;
   Insensitivity
Illiteracy, 98-99
Implied consent, 120
   See also Informed consent
Incompetence
   attorneys and, 2
   expert witnesses and, 158-
      159
   malpractice and, 1
   nurses and, 70-73
   See also Competency
Indifference
   malpractice suits and, 12-14
   See also Callousness
Informed consent, 95-102
   alternative treatment and,
      99-100
   distraught patients and, 98

employees and, 95-96
judgements in scope of
consent, 100-101
language barriers and, 98-99
rushing in, 96-97
sedated patients and, 98
self-protective advice in,
101-102
See also Implied consent
Insensitivity
communication and, 14-15
humor and, 11-12
malpractice suits and, 9-10
See also Callousness;
Indifference
Insurance companies. *See*
Health insurance;
Malpractice insurance
International Association of
Insurance Counsel, 166
Investigation
benefits of, 123-128
countersuits and, 195
expert witnesses, 163-164
technology and, 209-210
trial preparation and, 146
See also Private
investigators

Jokes. *See* Humor
Judges, 169-172
bias of, 170
functions of, 170-171
removal of, 169-170
treatment of, 171-172
Julian, Alfred, 13-14, 34
Juries, 173-177
abilities of, 177
contributory negligence
and, 153
denigrating the plantiff
and, 176-177
expert witnesses and, 158,
161
judges and, 169-170

medical testimony
and, 174
medications and, 83, 84
physician-defendant,
relationship with, 174-175
sensitivity to, 175-176

Karp, David, 54, 108

Laboratory tests
colleague communication
and, 57-58
diagnostic errors and, 76-77
medical records and, 94
reporting of, 16-17
See also Diagnosis
Language barriers, 98-99
Lawyers. *See* Attorney
(physician's); Attorney
(plaintiff's)
Learnard, John N., 64, 66
Legal costs, 32-33, 197-198
Legal precedent. *See*
Precedent
Letters of apology, 198

Malice requirement
(countersuits), 196-197
Malingerers (patient type),
37-38
Malpractice insurance
communication with
plantiff's lawyer and, 146
general settlements and,
58-59
going without, 31-34
lawyer assignment by, 135
Preferred Provider
Organizations and, 203
settlement and, 137-138
understanding the policy,
27-30
witness files of, 165-166
Medical advice
patient disregard of, 4-5

termination of services and,
25
See also Patient compliance
Medical education
(continuing), 205-206
Medical Liability Mutual
Insurance Company of
New York, 168
Medical records, 89-94
alterations of, 91-92, 146
demonstrative evidence
and, 181-182
deposition and, 143
emergency rooms and, 110
good intentions in, 93-94
importance of, 89-90
indiscretions in, 90
laboratory tests and, 94
messiness in, 92-93
privileged material and, 90-
91
testimony and, 186
See also Documentation
Medicare
Diagnostic-Related Groups
and, 203
fraud and, 121
Medication, 81-87
administration of drug and,
85-86
birth defects and, 211
documentation and, 87
dosage and, 86
emergency room queries
and, 110
handwriting and, 86-87
prescription manner and,
82-83
side-effects/allergic
reactions and, 83-85
Michaud, Frederick C., 115,
116
Misunderstandings, 6-7
See also Communication
Multiple-defendant cases,
210

News media, 147
Nosocomial infections, 69
Nurses
expert testimony and, 208
liability and, 70-73
medications and, 85-86
physician relationship with,
72-73

Obstetrics, 210-211
Occurence coverage
insurance, 28
Oral informed consent, 102
See also Informed consent
Overwork, 15-16

Partnerships, 56-57
See also Group practice;
Solo practice
Patient compliance
contributory negligence
and, 151-155
documentation and, 4-5
termination of services and,
25
warning signs, 37-38
Patient's family. *See* Family
(patient's)
Patient types, 35-39
Pediatrics
diagnosis and, 78
family involvement and, 45
increase of suits in, 211
Pharmacists, 86-87
Pharmacology. *See*
Medication
Physician-nurse relationship,
72-73
See also Nurses
Postponements, 148-149
Precedents, 147
Preferred Provider
Organizations (PPOs),
202-203
Privacy. *See* Confidentiality;
Privileged information

Private investigators, 129-133
See also Investigation
Privileged information
defense attorney and, 146
medical records and, 90-91
See also Confidentiality
Procedure explanations, 44-
45
Pure loss coverage, 28-29

Questions (cross-
examination), 188-190

Reception (of patient), 48-49
Reckless abandon, 196-197
See also Abandonment
Referrals
contributory negligence
and, 153
emergency rooms and, 107-
111
importance of, 206-207
liability and, 55-56
Preferred Provider
Organizations (PPOs)
and, 202
See also Consultation
Refusal of treatment
hospitals, 62, 63, 64-65, 67
malpractice liability and,
23-24
Relatives. *See* Family
(patient's); Family
(physician's)
Reporting requirements, 29-
30
Research, 209-210
Revenge motive, 2-4
Rubsamen, David S., 106

Second opinions, 103-106
See also Consultation
Sedated patients, 98
Settlements
attorney selection and, 137-
138

plaintiff's lawyer and, 147
"Shotgun" cases, 210
Side effects (medication), 83-
85
Solo practice, 55-56. *See also*
Group practice;
Partnerships
Staff. *See* Employees
State medical societies, 198
Subpoenas, 139-140

Tape recordings, 102
See also Videotapes
Team approach, 210
Technology, 209-210
Telephone
etiquette for, 49
guidelines for, 113-117
reception and, 48
Testimony, 157-162
See also Expert witnesses
Testimony (physician-
defendant's), 183-192
anger and, 191
cross-examination, 187-192
direct examination, 185-
187
entry, 183-185
exit, 192
trial preparation, 147-148
Tests. *See* Diagnosis;
Laboratory tests
Time limits
informed consent and, 96-
97
insurance policies and, 29-
30
Tough talk. *See* Callousness;
Indifference;
Insensitivity
Transfers, 111
Treatment refusal. *See*
Refusal of treatment
Treatment withdrawal. *See*
Withdrawal of treatment
Trial preparation, 145-149

attorneys and, 145-147, 148
communication and, 146-
147
postponements and, 148-
149
testimony and, 147-148

Ultimate net loss coverage,
28-29
United States Department of
Health and Human
services, 76
Unnecessary procedures, 105

Videotapes
demonstrative evidence,
181-182
depositions, 209
See also Tape recordings
Visual evidence, 179-182

Waiting time, 49, 50
Walkup, Bruce, 14-15, 121-
122
Warning signs, 35-39
complainers, 36-37
cynics, 38
experts, 37
family and, 45
flattery, 35-36
grievers, 38-39
malingerers, 37-38
Warranty. *See* Guarantees
Weil, William, S., 121
Wise, Burton L., 167
Withdrawal of treatment, 23,
24-25
See also Abandonment
Witnesses
informed consent, 102
See also Expert witnesses